PRACTICAL GARDENING

CONTAINERS

PRACTICAL GARDENING

CONTAINERS

DAVID SQUIRE

JG PRESS

Published in the USA in 1995 by

JG PRESS

Distributed by

WORLD PUBLICATIONS, INC.

The JG Press imprint is a trademark of JG Press, Inc.

455 Somerset Avenue, North Dighton, MA 02764

Designed and produced by

THE BRIDGEWATER BOOK COMPANY

Art Director and Designer Terry Jeavons

Managing Editor Anna Clarkson

Series Editor Penny David

Illustrator Vana Haggerty

Studio photography Guy Ryecart *assisted by Jim Clowes*

Location photography Steve Wooster *assisted by Carolyn Clegg*

Typesetting and page make up Mark Woodhams

ISBN 1-57215-026-2

Produced by Mandarin Offset

Printed and bound in China

INTRODUCTION *6–11*

WINDOW BOXES AND TROUGHS *12–43*

HANGING BASKETS AND WALL BASKETS *44–67*

TUBS, POTS, URNS AND PLANTERS *68–93*

ORNAMENTAL PLANT GAZETTEER *94–107*

GLOSSARY *108–109*   INDEX *110–112*

INTRODUCTION

Growing plants in containers brings a new dimension to gardening, revitalizing dull areas and introducing colour and interest. Instant colour, quick-change colour schemes and a wide and varied repertoire of plants and containers have created a facet of gardening that each year increases in popularity.

Containers bring the garden on to patios, terraces and balconies, and when secured to walls or window sills introduce a vertical element. Free-standing containers, such as urns and tubs, can be used to flank flights of steps with colour, to make focal points in lawns or to add height. Pairs of containers at either side of entrances add importance and convey a welcoming message.

Containers can be colourful throughout the year; in summer they are usually ablaze with half-hardy annuals; during spring, bulbs produce magnificent displays; while in autumn and winter there are hardy evergreens and miniature conifers for permanent interest.

CHOOSING PLANTS

Urns, tubs and planters stand on suitable flat surfaces such as walls and patios, while window boxes, wall baskets and hanging baskets adorn vertical surfaces and are displayed at a height. It is therefore essential to choose appropriate plants for each type, both to show off the plants to perfection and to suit the container.

Trailing and cascading plants are essential for hanging baskets, wall baskets and the fronts of window boxes, while upright types are ideal for tubs and urns. Bear your container in mind when selecting plants from the range described throughout this book. Keep in mind, too, the colour of the background against which they will be seen. Mixing and arranging plants in containers so that their colours compliment one another and the setting can add enormously to the impact and enjoyment of a container display.

ABOVE Small containers brimming with flowers and foliage will fill every corner with colour and interest.
OPPOSITE A colourful feast of colour, combining foliage plants and summer-flowering bedding plants, is created using attractive troughs, window boxes and urns set at different heights.

ATTENTION TO DETAIL

Growing plants in containers demands regular care and attention. Where plants are grown in borders, the large volume of soil available to them ensures that if watering is neglected for a week or so there is still a reserve of moisture available. But when plants are in containers the amount of compost is relatively small and likely to dry out rapidly if not regularly watered. Feeding and dead-heading are also essential and these tasks, together with other practical information, are detailed on pages 20 and 21.

Container gardening is a pastime for everyone, whatever their age and agility. Indeed, many disabled gardeners find planting and looking after plants in tubs and window boxes quite within their ability, provided the patio's surface is flat and even. When planning a patio it is wise to design it with your old age in mind.

RANGE OF CONTAINERS

The range of containers for displaying on patios, terraces and around houses is huge. It includes not only purpose-made, ornamental items such as hanging baskets, wall baskets, window boxes, troughs, tubs and urns, but also more unexpected items such as sinks, old wheelbarrows, tyres and growing-bags. Indeed, the scope for originality and novelty is near boundless; if a container can hold sufficient suitable compost to support plants, it becomes a candidate for creating anything from a splash of colour as a focal point on a lawn or patio to a garden in microcosm.

Some of the larger containers, like tubs and window boxes, create homes for plants throughout the year. Hanging baskets are best reserved for summer performances, although these need not be confined to conventional ornamentals: you can plant them with low-growing, cascading roses, or with attractive and succulent strawberries and tomatoes.

It is the excitement of growing plants in non-orthodox ways that appeals to many gardeners, and throughout this book we show a wide spectrum of traditional and non-traditional containers and treatments.

TUBS AND URNS

These traditional, purpose-made containers are used to grow a wide range of plants, some permanently, others just during summer.

Tubs provide plants with plenty of compost, so shrubs, small trees and dwarf or slow-growing conifers are left in them throughout the year. The tubs tend to be permanent.

Urns are usually more decorative in character. They also hold less compost, and so are more suited to ephemeral plants, including annuals, planted just for their summer flowering season. Urns can be displayed on plinths or at ground level, but are often used to enhance architecture – they look good positioned at the top or bottom of a flight of steps.

Fuchsia 'Jack Shahan'

Impatiens 'Elfin Mixed'

LEFT Window boxes and troughs planted with bulbs and biennials become awash with colour in spring and early summer. Choose varieties carefully to ensure that combinations of plants harmonize with each other, as well as with their backgrounds. Throughout this book, mixing and matching plants is discussed, as well as choosing combinations that are particularly suited to different settings. Considering these factors usually costs no more than just buying plants at random – and generally produces far more rewarding results. Here is a combination of daffodils and polyanthus.

Yellow *Begonia* 'Non Stop'

Lysimachia

Petunia 'Surfina'

Lobelia 'Colour Fountain Mix'

ABOVE Hanging baskets are beacons of colour during summer, tightly packed with bushy and trailing half-hardy annuals raised earlier in the year in gentle warmth. Tender perennial plants can also be used, such as cascading fuchsias. Certain varieties of tomatoes, cucumbers, peppers and strawberries are also good candidates for hanging baskets.

HANGING BASKETS AND WALL BASKETS

These are traditional containers for displaying summer-flowering plants. Hanging baskets are positioned to introduce colour at eye-height to walls and the sides of entrances, while wall baskets (which resemble hanging baskets cut in half) are also superb when secured at waist-height to walls. Small mangers are an alternative, with a more rural appearance than wall baskets.

WINDOW BOXES AND TROUGHS

Window boxes are generally secured to window-sills or to the area of wall just below a window. Troughs can be at ground level, raised on short legs, on top of a wall or at the side of a flat roof.

By using three different inner containers and rotating them – winter, spring and summer – it is possible to create quick-change colour throughout the year.

STONE SINKS

These are ideal for positioning on patios and planting with small rock-garden plants, miniature bulbs and small conifers. Shallow, stone sinks are best, but white, glazed types can be modified and made very attractive (*see pages 82 and 83*).

WHEELBARROWS

Old wooden wheelbarrows provide ideal homes for summer-flowering plants. Metal types also can be used, but in summer the compost in them warms up dramatically unless fully clothed with leaves and flowers. Regular watering is imperative.

ABOVE The range of plants that can be grown in containers is wide and includes bulbs, summer-flowering bedding plants and small-scale topiary. Many long-lived houseplants grown for their attractive foliage can also be placed outdoors during summer, and this is especially useful in warm, sheltered areas.

ABOVE An old metal wheelbarrow creates an unusual container for summer-flowering bedding plants. During the summer they can also be filled with some of the hardier houseplants.

BELOW A shallow stone sink enables many small alpine plants and miniature bulbs to be grown and displayed on a patio. Miniature conifers can also be used and these introduce height and permanency to the display. These features create interest throughout the entire year.

RANGE OF MATERIALS

The materials used to create containers for plants includes wood, concrete, lead and other metals, reconstituted stone, plastic and glassfibre. Each material has its advantages and disadvantages, but the essence is that any container made from it should be able to sustain plants, nutritionally and physically. It must have holes in its base for excess moisture to escape. It should be strong enough to support the weight of compost, and able to survive the rigours of frost, rain, snow and sunshine. It must also remain cool so that compost does not warm up excessively in summer. In some gardens it may have to be solid enough to survive the buffeting of winds, boisterous children or dogs. Above all, it should be attractive, so that you enjoy looking at it and gardening in it.

ABOVE This stone urn, fashioned into a basket with animal feet, is filled with a single variety of begonias with bright-red flowers and green and cream variegated leaves.

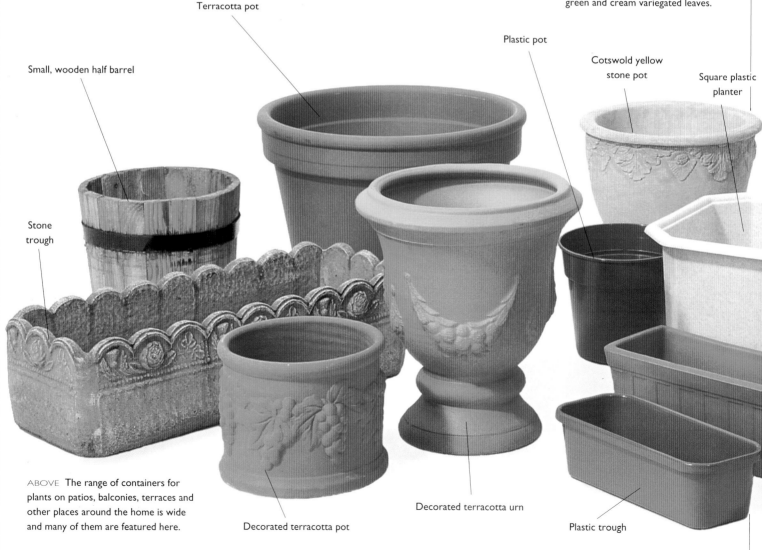

Terracotta pot

Plastic pot

Cotswold yellow stone pot

Square plastic planter

Small, wooden half barrel

Stone trough

Decorated terracotta urn

Plastic trough

Decorated terracotta pot

ABOVE The range of containers for plants on patios, balconies, terraces and other places around the home is wide and many of them are featured here.

MATERIAL FACTORS

Containers made from some traditional materials such as lead are rare and expensive, but versatile synthetics such as plastic and glassfibre can offer good quality reproductions more cheaply.

Wood is a traditional material with the merit of insulating compost from cold temperatures in winter and heat in summer. It is used to make barrels and tubs as well as window boxes and troughs. It can be painted or varnished, or left to weather naturally.

Reconstituted stone is now a popular material for containers as well as statues and garden ornaments. It has brought the possibility of classically styled stone-type urns, pots, vases and troughs within the budget of more gardeners. In texture, this material resembles Portland stone but weathers and mellows quicker. Reconstituted stone can be cleaned by using plenty of water and a soft brush – do not use a stiff wire brush as this will scratch the surface. Take care not to knock or drop containers formed from it.

Wood and stone are, perhaps, the most natural looking materials.

LEFT Tall pots and wall-hung planters enable plants to be displayed at varying heights. Plants in their own pots can just be positioned in the tops of larger pots so that the display can be quickly changed and, perhaps, slightly tender plants returned indoors or into a greenhouse.

BELOW These containers enable a wide range of plants to be grown; tubs are ideal for permanent plants such as small shrubs and miniature conifers, while troughs and window boxes create homes for spring-flowering bulbs and summer-brightening half-hardy annuals.

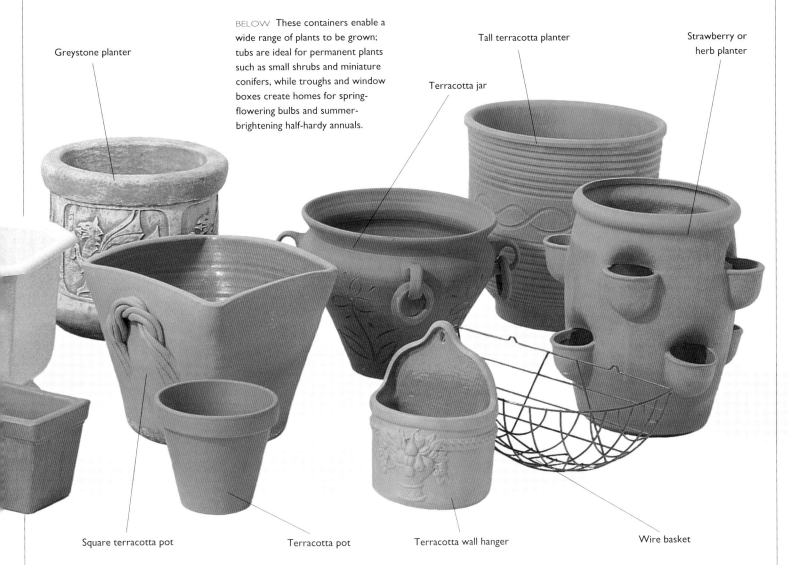

Greystone planter

Tall terracotta planter

Terracotta jar

Strawberry or herb planter

Square terracotta pot

Terracotta pot

Terracotta wall hanger

Wire basket

WINDOW BOXES AND TROUGHS

Window boxes transform windows throughout the year. At one time, they were filled with plants only in summer; the rest of the year they were packed away in a shed or just left barren of colour. They are usually at their most colourful during summer when clothed in bright flowers. In winter they are mainly planted with small evergreen shrubs and trailers, often variegated, with miniature bulbs creating extra colour in late winter and early spring. In mid- and late spring, daffodils and tulips combine with biennials to produce a bright picture. Troughs can be given the same yearly cycle of plants as window boxes.

Window boxes are secured to window sills or an area of wall just below, while troughs have a wide range of uses. They can be secured to walls and roofs, positioned at ground level, or slightly raised on short legs. And as well as creating homes for outdoor plants, when placed in lobbies and porches they are ideal for less hardy plants.

DESIGN AND DIMENSIONS

Wood is the most common material used for window boxes and troughs. A window box should be no more than 90cm (3ft) long, and preferably only 75cm (2½ft). This is because window boxes and troughs over this length become too heavy to lift when filled with plants and moist compost and may break under the weight. For wider sills, use two containers. The wood can be painted to suit the plants.

Terracotta outer containers have a texture and colour that naturally harmonizes with plants. Because of their weight, position these containers either on strong, concrete or brick window sills, or use at ground level as a trough.

Reconstituted stone is also heavy and therefore best

ABOVE Window boxes should be designed so that they do not prevent windows being opened.
OPPOSITE Troughs at ground level can create a magnificent display. During summer, summer-flowering bedding plants can be used, with bulbs in spring and miniature conifers and variegated shrubs in winter.

positioned at ground level. Its surface has a natural, stone-like appearance and soon mellows. Concrete troughs are suitable only for use at ground level.

Glassfibre is durable, light and rot-proof, and comes in a range of finishes, some smooth, others more rustic. Glassfibre containers make ideal window boxes and troughs. Although they are strong, do not to drop them.

Plastic is an all-embracing term and encompasses materials of many degrees of thickness, durability and life expectancy. Plastic is ideal as inner boxes for troughs and window boxes.

Recycled cellulose fibre troughs are ideal as inexpensive but short-lived inner containers. They can also be used on their own along the edge of a flat roof.

USING WINDOW BOXES

The simplest and easiest way to use a window box is just to plant summer-flowering half-hardy annuals in it during late spring and to put it outside as soon as all risk of frost is over – often not until early summer in some temperate climates. This is fine for summer displays, but is not imaginative and does not get the best from a window box.

To extend the season of interest, choose a window box with a trough-like box that fits inside. If you get three separate inner containers, you can plan a series of plantings for spring, summer and winter to make the window box attractive all year round.

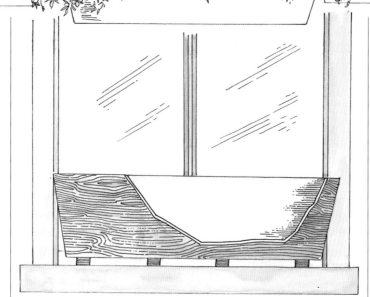

Spring-flowering displays are formed of bulbous and biennial plants. These displays are planted in autumn.

Summer-flowering displays are mainly formed of half-hardy annuals. They are planted in late spring.

Winter displays are left in their inner containers and from spring to autumn given a cool, shady position.

SPRING DISPLAYS

These are mainly created by bulbs and biennials which burst into colour from early to late spring and sometimes continue into early summer. An inner box is planted with these in late summer or early autumn, the compost watered and the container placed in a cool, sheltered position until early spring, by which time the bulbs will have produced leaves and buds that will soon produce a magnificent display.

The winter display is then removed from the window box and the spring one put in instead. Place the container holding the winter display in a cool, shaded position during summer and regularly check that the compost is moist. Raise the container on bricks to discourage the entry of slugs and snails, which can soon decimate plants.

ABOVE By rotating spring, summer and winter displays in plastic inner window boxes, it is possible to create colour at the bases of windows throughout the year. Also, using these containers prevents wooden window boxes from rotting through constant direct contact with excessively wet compost. Indeed, every time a display is changed in a wooden outer window box, check that the wood is sound. Ensure that there are holes in its base to allow water draining into it from the inner box to escape quickly and freely.

SUMMER DISPLAYS

These are mainly formed of half-hardy annuals. Other suitable plants include pelargoniums, fuchsias and tuberous-rooted begonias. The range of half-hardy annuals suitable for planting in window boxes is extensive and each year further varieties are offered by seed companies and nurseries.

They are all quickly damaged by frost and therefore cannot be placed outside until all risk of frost has passed. Containers holding these plants can be planted during late spring and early summer and placed outside during the day. While there is any threat of frost, they must be put in a frost-proof greenhouse or conservatory at night.

In warm areas, where frost is a rarity, it is possible to place them in position outside during mid- or even early spring, whereas in extremely cold regions the first week in early summer is the earliest possible date.

As soon as the weather becomes suitable, remove the spring-flowering display from the container and carefully put the summer one in its place.

Place the container holding the spring display in a cool position and gradually allow the compost to become dry. Pull out and discard biennial plants such as wallflowers, and allow the foliage of bulbs to die down naturally. Later, remove the bulbs and plant them around shrubs or naturalize them in lawns or on banks.

Some gardeners tend to leave bulbs in the container from one season to another, but to ensure a good display each year it is much better to remove them and replace them with fresh, healthy, good-sized bulbs.

WINTER DISPLAYS

These are placed in window boxes as soon as the summer display has finished. The exact timing varies and depends on the weather; also, if summer-flowering plants have been fed, watered and dead-headed regularly, their flowering period is extended. But eventually cool nights will curtail growth.

Winter displays are often left in the container for several years, until plants need to be divided or become too large. An annual top-up of fresh compost keeps them healthy. Suitable plants include miniature conifers, small shrubs, winter-flowering heathers and small-leaved and variegated ivies. Miniature bulbs that flower in late winter can also be used and these too can be left in position for several years.

When a winter display becomes congested and needs replanting, tackle this task in spring, so that plants have the complete summer in which to become established before being replaced in the window box in early autumn. However, if including small, winter-flowering bulbs – such as winter aconite *(Eranthis hyemalis)* – delay replanting until late summer, when fresh bulbs become available from garden centres and high street shops.

ABOVE For casement windows, where windows are hinged at their sides and open outwards over the sill, place the window box on brackets secured to the wall below the sill. Even so, it is likely that the flowers will eventually prevent windows being open fully. However, for sash windows it is possible to position the window box directly on the sill.

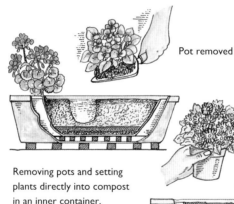

Pot removed

Removing pots and setting plants directly into compost in an inner container.

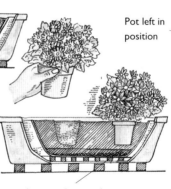

Pot left in position

Leaving plants in their pots and standing them in moist peat in an inner container.

ABOVE Plants can be put into window boxes in two ways. The first is to plant them directly into compost in an inner plastic trough. The trough has pea-shingle in its base, then a layer of peat to assist in the retention of moisture. Compost is then added. Partly fill the trough with compost, at the same time setting the plants in place after removing them from their pots. After planting is complete, the surface of the compost should be about 12mm (½ in) below the trough's rim. This space allows the compost to be watered; if too small, it is difficult to add sufficient water.

The second way of planting window boxes is to stand the plants together with their pots in the inner plastic trough and surround them with moist peat. This method is often used for plants in lobbies and porches. It enables those that have finished flowering to be quickly changed. Ensure that the surface of each pot is about 12mm (½ in) below the trough's rim. The compost in the pots is watered individually, according to its dryness.

Use strong brackets and sound wall fixings when securing a window box to a wall beneath a window. As well as supporting the window box, each bracket must have a lip to prevent the box slipping and falling off. This is especially important where window boxes are at the front of a house and directly over a public thoroughfare. Ensure the window box is level; if uneven, water flows to one end and the compost does not remain uniformly moist. Secure one bracket to the wall, then use a spirit level to ensure the second one is horizontal.

Always use galvanized screws. Steel screws rust and cause stains on walls, especially unsightly on light colours like white or grey.

USING TROUGHS

Troughs are versatile and can be featured in many ways in gardens as well as on patios, terraces and balconies. By selecting suitable plants they also can be used in porches and lobbies. The choice of material for your trough depends partly on what style you want, but partly on factors such as size and weight, and where you intend to position it. Reconstituted stone troughs are heavy and therefore best used at ground level or on stout low walls. Terracotta is a relatively heavy material, with a natural affinity for brickwork surroundings, among others. Wood is usually lighter in weight, and this versatile, natural material blends well into many styles of garden, as well making a good foil for plants. Glassfibre is durable and light, so is particularly useful on roofs and balconies. Both modern styles and reproductions of traditional designs and materials are available. Plastic troughs have a limited life especially when positioned in strong sunlight, but make inexpensive short-term homes to display annuals for a season or two.

ABOVE A large, raised trough presents the opportunity to create a medley of foliage plants, some permanent, with others just added for summer. This trough creates a home for variegated phormiums, together with several agaves which need the comfort of a frost-proof greenhouse or conservatory in winter in temperate regions.

SUPPORTING TROUGHS

Most troughs used in gardens have flat bases. The trough is either raised off the ground on 2.5cm (1in) square pieces of wood, positioned on top of a wall or flat roof, or secured by brackets against a wall. For troughs displayed on patios, it is an advantage to have short legs. The added height enables trailing plants to be freely used around their sides. The legs, additionally, help to prevent slugs and snails reaching plants. Young, soft plants can soon be devastated by these garden pests.

WALL DISPLAYS

Troughs look good secured either to the top or side of a wall. For the top of a wall 90cm–1.2m (3–4ft) high, use a heavy trough – made of reconstituted stone or terracotta – and select mainly low-growing or trailing plants. This limits the area exposed to strong winds which rapidly dry out compost.

If the wall is low – 75cm (2½ft) or less – plastic and glassfibre troughs can be used as the weight of compost will prevent it falling off.

For troughs secured to the sides of walls, use strong wall brackets with lips. There, tall and bushy plants, as well as climbing and trailing types, will create a large area of colour. The sides of walls give protection and enable slightly fewer plants to be grown.

ROOF DISPLAYS

The edges of flat roofs on garages and home extensions often look dreary. They can be brightened by placing troughs about 10cm (4in) in from the side and planting them with summer-flowering bedding plants of short, bushy habit, mixed with some trailing ones. Ensure the trough has a smooth base, with no sharp corners to damage the roof.

Water the compost regularly to ensure it remains moist. Adding perlite or vermiculite to the compost helps in the retention of moisture. To aid watering, extension arms to hosepipes allow troughs to be watered without you having to stand on steps or ladders. Alternatively, tie a hosepipe to a bamboo pole and bend over the end; a piece of wire helps to keep it in position.

RIGHT Reconstituted stone troughs supported by ornate legs give a feeling of age and permanency. They can be planted with flowering as well as foliage plants.

PAVED AREAS

Troughs to brighten patio edges can stand at ground level or be placed on a low balustrade or wall. Rather than positioning flat-bottomed troughs directly on the patio's surface, raise them slightly on 2.5cm (1in) square pieces of wood.

For troughs placed at ground level, choose bright-faced, upright plants. For those raised on low walls, choose trailing and sprawling varieties as well as a few bushy types, so that the wall below becomes drenched in colour. For a trough backed by a wall, consider climbers as well as taller growing plants.

BELOW Troughs on balconies are superb when positioned close to the edge, allowing trailing plants to cascade through the railings; they help to soften the angular lines of the balcony. Troughs also look good when positioned at the base of a wall, and here plants with a more upright and bushy nature should be used. There are many summer-flowering plants to choose from, including fuchsias, busy Lizzies, ageratums and pelargoniums. Variegated plants can also be used.

BRIGHTENING SUMMER-HOUSES

Troughs, together with window boxes, are ideal for introducing colour to the exterior of summer-houses and sheds. Both bushy and trailing plants are ideal, but ensure that when the plants are watered no drips fall on wood, causing staining or decay. Regular watering is essential, especially if the trough is under a widely overhanging eave or roof.

WHITE BACKGROUNDS

White walls and fences enhance the drama of rich, brightly coloured flowers such as red, scarlet, yellow, gold, dark-blue and deep-mauve. A display of all-green and variegated foliage can also look attractive, with the green and white colour combination creating a cool and refreshing feel – this would be particularly appealing set against the painted white walls of a south-facing patio or back yard. White backgrounds are especially dominant when in strong sunlight.

Fuchsia 'Patio Princess'

Geranium 'Pac Laura'

Begonia 'Happy Choice Mixed'

Geranium 'Orbit Pink'

Pelargonium 'L'Elegante'

Tagetes 'Bonanza Mixed'

Fuchsia 'Jack Shahan'

Fuchsia 'Brutus'

Verbena 'Norans Mixed'

Ageratum 'Pacific'

ABOVE Troughs on legs enable slightly trailing, as well as bushy and upright plants, to be grown. In addition to summer-flowering bedding plants, both ivy-leaved pelargoniums and small-leaved variegated ivies can be used along the edges.

COMPOSTS AND PLANTING

Well-drained yet moisture-retentive compost is essential for all plants in containers. This may appear to be a contradiction in terms, but it can be achieved by using the compost mixture suggested on this page.

The planting medium must also be fertile for summer-flowering bedding plants, which need to develop rapidly and to sustain growth throughout the long months of summer.

Spring-flowering bulbs – which are planted in late summer or autumn – do not need high fertility, as each one of them is a store-house of concentrated energy and a good display of flowers is assured.

Too much plant food at the wrong time can be detrimental to winter displays; they are best given a feed in late spring or early summer, but certainly not long after mid-summer. Young shoots that develop late in summer may be too tender to survive winter in exposed areas.

SUITABLE COMPOSTS

Use a mixture of equal parts loam-based and peat-based compost. The peat part retains moisture, in particular, while the loam-based part provides nutrients, especially the minor ones. The addition of perlite or vermiculite further assists in the retention of moisture.

Impatiens 'Starbright Mixed'

SUMMER DISPLAYS

1 Summer-flowering displays become packed with colour from early summer to the frosts of autumn. To ensure success, the compost must be fertile and able to retain moisture. If it dries out, plants are soon damaged and may not fully recover. Select an inner, plastic trough and, if it has been used before, remove all debris and wash thoroughly. Place broken crocks (pieces of clay pots), concave side downwards, over the drainage holes, then a layer of clean, well-washed pea-shingle and a further one of moist peat. Compost is then put on top.

2 Initially, place only a small amount of compost over the peat. This allows for pot-plants with large root-balls to be planted without having to use a trowel to dig away vast amounts of compost. As each plant is positioned, pack and firm compost around the roots. Do not bury plants too deeply. Plants raised in seed trays will not have large, firm root-balls; handle them carefully.

3 Position large plants to the back of the trough and small and trailing ones at the front, but bear in mind that displays with an irregular outline are usually more interesting than those that form an even and level top. Check that the compost is about 12mm ($\frac{1}{2}$ in) below the rim, then thoroughly water the compost. Try not to moisten leaves and flowers excessively. Allow surplus moisture to drain before putting the trough in the outer box.

BELOW The permutations of summer-flowering plants for planting in both window boxes and troughs is wide and each year seed companies introduce further ones. Additionally, slightly tender plants from indoors can be introduced to the display, but if they have a perennial nature they will have to be returned indoors or into a greenhouse or conservatory before the onset of frosts.

Geranium
'Challenge Pink'

Nicotiana
'Domino Pink'

Begonia
'Non Stop'

Tagetes
'Bonanza'

Fuchsia
'Rose Winston'

WINTER DISPLAYS

1 Winter displays are filled with hardy plants, including miniature conifers, small-flowering or variegated shrubs and trailers such as small-leaved ivies. Because winter displays are created from established plants, you can arrange them in an attractive way before putting them in the inner trough.

2 Fill the container in the same way as suggested on page 18 for summer displays. Half fill the container with compost, then remove each pot and place the plants in the trough (*below*). Ensure the top of each soil-ball is about 12mm (½in) below the trough's rim. If positioned too deep, the foliage may be spoilt.

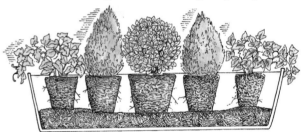

3 Use your fingers to pack and firm compost around each soil-ball (*right*). Level off the surface and carefully water the compost. Do not use strong jets of water, as this will disturb the surface and may push compost to one end of the container. Allow stems and leaves of trailing plants to cascade freely along the front and sides of the box.

SPRING DISPLAYS

When planting bulbs for spring displays, set each bulb to about three times its own depth. If a bulb is planted excessively deeply, the development of shoots in spring will be retarded or even prevented. A bulb planted too shallowly, on the other hand, may be damaged by cold temperatures during winter. Also, if not sufficiently deep, the plant will not be well-anchored in the compost and may topple over.

WATERING, FEEDING AND CARE

Watering, feeding and looking after plants in window boxes is essential. Summer-flowering bedding plants need more attention than spring and winter displays. During summer, watering is a prime need and if this is erratic or neglected for long periods plants soon die. Feeding is also essential, as well as removing dead flowers.

Bulbs are more self-reliant and when planted in good compost produce a colourful display without further assistance. Once planted in well-drained compost, winter displays need little care, other than a feed during late spring and in mid-summer.

Weeding the compost is also essential. If weeds are neglected, plants can eventually become suffocated. Weeds also encourage the presence of pests and diseases.

WATERING

The relatively small volume of compost and large number of plants in window boxes make it essential to water the compost regularly during summer and to keep it evenly moist at other times of the year – but without causing it to become continually waterlogged.

The selection of a good moisture-retentive compost is vital (*see pages 18 and 19*).

1 Often, window boxes at ground level are surrounded by pots and tubs which make it difficult to reach for watering. To make watering easier, tie the end of a hosepipe to a 1.2m (4ft) long cane and slowly dribble water on the compost.

2 Window boxes secured on the sill of sash-type windows can be easily reached from inside the house. This is especially useful when a window box is at an upper-storey window. Try to avoid dropping excessive moisture on the leaves and flowers.

3 When window boxes are secured under upstairs windows or positioned on roofs there is always the temptation to stand on a rickety garden stool to water them or just to spray water over the plants. Neither is good: there is a chance that the stool will slip; and spraying leaves will not adequately moisten the compost. The solution is to use a ladder or step-ladder, or to buy a proprietary lance-like attachment to a hosepipe so that a slow trickle of water can be applied to the compost.

DEAD-HEADING

Regularly removing dead flowers encourages the development of further buds and prolongs the display. Besides, blooms left on plants decay and encourage the onset of diseases. Where plants have long flower stalks, cut these back to the base. Where flowers are borne in tight clusters close to the main stem, use scissors to cut them off. Pick up all dead flowers and place on a compost heap. If left among plants they encourage diseases.

Use sharp, pointed scissors to cut off individual flowers.

Cut off entire leaf-stalks where complete heads have faded.

FEEDING

The difference in growth, vitality and colour between summer-flowering bedding plants that are fed regularly and those that are neglected is remarkable. If plants are left to rely totally on nutrients in the compost, by mid-summer they will have exhausted it. The compost then becomes a mass of roots searching for food.

There are several ways to apply nutrients: the most common method is a liquid, but there are also granular and powder types and nutrient sticks which are just pushed into the compost.

1 A liquid fertilizer is the most widely used and convenient way of feeding plants. In this form, it is readily available for absorption by the plants. Always dilute concentrated liquid fertilizer according to the instructions on the bottle. Making it stronger may not only damage plants but can eventually produce compost that is toxic to them. Carefully measure the concentrated fertilizer into the correct amount of fresh water and agitate with a clean stick. Always use a clean watering-can when feeding plants.

2 Sticks and pills of concentrated plant fertilizer are increasingly popular and provide nutrients over a long period. They are clean and quick to use, but the chemicals are not so readily available to plants as those applied in water. They are suitable only for summer-flowering plants.

3 Granular and powdered fertilizers are more widely used in gardens, where they can be dusted on the soil's surface, lightly hoed in and then watered. The only way to use them for feeding plants in containers is to dissolve them thoroughly in clean water first. Agitate the mixture and immediately apply it to the compost. Ensure that the liquid does not fall on leaves and flowers.

LEFT Feeding plants regularly is an essential part of creating a bright and continuous display of flowers during summer, whether in troughs, window boxes, hanging baskets or pots. These plants soon exhaust compost of its nutrients and if the task of feeding is neglected by mid-summer the display may look very dismal. Liquid fertilizers are the most common way to apply food to plants, but sticks and pills as well as granular and powdered types can be used.

BELOW Regular watering and feeding is essential to ensure a long-lasting and dramatic display of blooms in summer.

WHEN TO FEED PLANTS

Not all plants in window boxes need regular feeding.

✳ Summer-flowering bedding plants need feeding regularly from early to late summer, at about three-week intervals.

✳ Spring-flowering displays formed of bulbs and biennials like wallflowers and daisies do not need to be fed. But do use fresh and fertile compost.

✳ Winter-flowering displays must not be fed between the beginning of late summer and late spring. When winter containers are enjoying their off-season break in a cool, shaded position, feed them in late spring and mid-summer.

SUMMER DISPLAYS IN WINDOW BOXES

Summer is a magical time in gardens and especially in window boxes, where colour is concentrated into a small area. Many flowering plants are suitable for these containers. You can make attractive, well-balanced compositions by choosing plants of different habits – some trailing and cascading, others bushy and upright.

Mixing and matching colours has infinite potential and enables gardeners to assume the role of a painter. Success depends not only on making interesting colour schemes using flowers and leaves, but on taking into account the colour tones in the background of the display. The colour and texture of the container, too, can be an important element in the final picture, often dramatically influencing the display.

SELECTING PLANTS

When buying plants, take the time to inspect them carefully to ensure that they will develop quickly and be healthy and become strong.

* Ensure they are free from pests and diseases. Always check under leaves.
* Do not buy lanky and spindly plants; stocky ones with short spaces between the leaves are much better.

* Check that the compost is moist; if dry, the plants will have received a check in growth and may not recover.
* Ensure the plants are labelled and of the variety you desire. The wrong variety will produce plants different in size and colour, radically changing the planned effect.
* Do not buy plants that are exceptionally congested and with matted roots.

ABOVE This brightly coloured summer-flowering window box is packed with petunias, nasturtiums, and trailing pelargoniums. The variegated castor oil plant positioned at the rear of the display is an unusual feature.

RIGHT These summer displays in window boxes are formed of flowering plants, variegated foliage and fully hardy small-leaved variegated ivies.

Geranium
'Gala' and 'Challenge'
varieties

Salvia
'Blaze of Glory'

Begonia
'Non Stop Mixed'

Tradescantia

New Guinea
Impatiens

MIXING AND MATCHING

The combinations of plants and colour schemes are vast and clearly a matter of personal choice. Here and on the following pages are medleys of plants to consider for window boxes:

✳ Trailing lobelia planted at the edges and front, zonal pelargoniums, sweet alyssum at the front, *Begonia × tuberhybrida* and large-faced summer-flowering pansies (*Viola × wittrockiana*).

ESTABLISHING PLANTS QUICKLY

After buying plants and getting them home, place them in a cool, lightly shaded position until they can be planted. If frost is expected at night, place them in a greenhouse or conservatory – or even indoors. Water the compost to ensure plants do not become desiccated. However, ensure that the compost does not become waterlogged.

Sketch out on a sheet of paper the approximate positions of all the different plants you have chosen. This often saves disturbing plants later after discovering they are too close together or in the wrong positions.

SPACING THE PLANTS

Plants grown in window boxes are generally planted closer together than those in flower-beds outdoors. This is because a more rapid and colour-packed display is desired. Nevertheless, do not pack them so close that within a month or so they are suffocating one another. If congestion becomes a problem, a few plants can be discreetly removed later, as long as this does not produce gaps that the other plants cannot fill within a week or so. But do not do this after mid-summer, as the plants will not then fill up the gaps. A liquid feed will soon create extra growth to fill any conspicuous gaps.

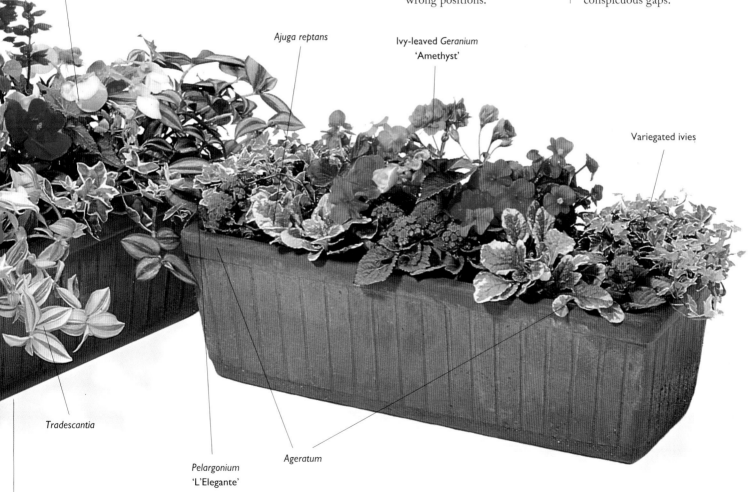

Begonia
'Non Stop'

Ajuga reptans

Ivy-leaved *Geranium*
'Amethyst'

Variegated ivies

Tradescantia

Pelargonium
'L'Elegante'

Ageratum

SUMMER FLOWER DISPLAYS

The permutations of flowering plants in window boxes is infinite and their selection depends on personal preference. The aim should be to cover the box with bushy and trailing plants that create dominant patches of colour. Avoid using too many different plants, or your window box will lack definition and form. A multi-mixture style may suit some gardeners, especially where there is only one window box. But where several windows each have a window box, simplicity and a display based on a repetition of perhaps just five different plants create the best effect.

FLOWERS FOR WINDOW BOXES

It is important to remember when selecting plants for window boxes that they need to look attractive when seen from both indoors and out. To achieve this, a series of low, bushy plants that will make mounds of colour along the top of the container is the first requirement. Intersperse these with plants that have sprawling or trailing flower stems which can be directed towards the front and sides of the box. This will help to soften its outline. Flowers can be used alone or mixed with various foliage plants (*see pages 26 to 29*).

FLOWER FORMS

As well as considering colour for summer window boxes, choose plants with contrasting flower shapes. Masses of tiny blooms, such as sweet alyssum and trailing lobelia, create a hazy effect. Larger flowers make splashes of distinct colour – tuberous begonias, petunias, godetias, busy Lizzies, pansies and pelargoniums, including the relatively new Continental or Swiss Balcon geraniums, all smother containers with flowers throughout summer. Other favourites include cascading and bushy fuchsias, salvias, mimulus, dwarf marigolds and ageratums.

Begonia 'Non Stop White'

Pansy 'Reveille Mixed'

Tradescantia 'Fluminensis'

MIXING AND MATCHING

Here are two superb combinations of plants for planting in summer window boxes:

✳ Marguerites (*Chrysanthemum frutescens*), trailing petunias cascading over the front and edges of the container, floss flower (*Ageratum houstonianum*), dwarf marigolds and ivy-leaved pelargoniums.

✳ Swiss Balcon pelargoniums (sometimes known as Continental geraniums), godetias, trailing and compact impatiens, ivy-leaved pelargoniums and *Kochia scoparia* 'Childsii' to add height to the display.

Campanula isophylla, wax begonias and low-growing tobacco plants are also popular. Slightly less often seen are *Nemesia strumosa compacta*,

Nemophilla menziesii 'Pennie Black', *Nemophilla maculata* '5-Spot', calceolarias, *Brachyscombe iberidifolia* 'Splendour', *Anagallis linifolia* 'Gentian Blue' and the increasingly popular and widely grown *Nieremabergia* 'Mont Blanc'. Many of these are detailed on pages 94 to 107.

Nicotiana 'Domino Pink'

Pansy 'Reveille Mixed'

Verbena 'Novalis Mixed'

Tradescantia 'Fluminensis'

Fuchsia 'Rose Winston'

ABOVE Summer-flowering displays in window boxes last until the frosts of autumn. Shown here is a mixture of begonias, trailing lobelia and busy Lizzies.

LEFT Wooden window boxes – especially when displayed in rural areas – can be given a more attractive outline by fixing strips of wood to them. Individualizing window boxes in this way was especially popular in Victorian times; some strips were positioned horizontally along the sides, other times vertically. Even thin strips of bark were used. Wooden troughs can also be enhanced in this way.

SUMMER FOLIAGE

Plants grown for their attractive foliage introduce further colours and textures to window boxes, and most have the advantage of lasting throughout summer and until the frosts of autumn. This is especially important in late summer when some flowers are beginning to fade, but a few foliage plants are an essential ingredient in many displays to act as a quiet foil for the more exuberant flower colours.

Foliage plants that are suitable for window boxes range from half-hardy annuals to those sufficiently hardy to be transferred from summer displays in autumn, planted into other containers and left outside. Small-leaved variegated ivies are an example of hardy types. The grey-leaved *Helichrysum petiolare* is not sufficiently hardy in temperate climates to be left outside during winter, while the half-hardy annual *Kochia scoparia* 'Childsii' naturally dies in autumn with the arrival of frosts.

FOLIAGE PLANTS
Although readily available and widely used in window boxes and other containers, small-leaved variegated ivies should not be discounted in any display. They are bright and remain attractive throughout summer, whatever the weather. They are ideal for trailing over the front and sides of a window box and available in many colour combinations.

The liquorice plant (*Helichrysum petiolare*) has cascading and arching stems peppered with roundish grey leaves covered with woolly hairs. Increasingly used is a yellow-leaved form, *H. p.* 'Aureum' or 'Limelight'. Both of these helichrysums can be raised from cuttings taken in mid- to late summer and overwintered in a frostproof greenhouse or conservatory.

RIGHT The ornate and aged appearance of this window box harmonizes with the foliage plants used in this summer display. The entire design has a restful appearance and is better suited for positioning on an old building than a stark and angular new one.

Pelargonium 'Lady Plymouth'

Peppermint-scented geranium

Variegated ivy

Helichrysum petiolatum

ABOVE Foliage plants with variegated or coloured leaves create a long-term display. Here the variegated ground ivy (*Glechoma hederacea* 'Variegata') and the yellow-leaved *Helichrysum petiolare* 'Aureum' soften the front edge of a window box, as well as harmonizing with white-and-yellow flowering plants.

RIGHT The delicately cut, fern-like leaves of *Senecio bicolor cineraria* 'Silver Dust' form a silvery-white mound throughout summer. It can be used mixed just with foliage plants, or as a background for flowering types. In sheltered areas it continues its display well into winter.

The aptly named dusty miller has deeply lobed leaves covered with white, woolly hairs that produce a silvery appearance. It is now known as *Senecio bicolor cineraria*, but an earlier name was *Cineraria maritima*. The variety 'Silver Dust' has bright, silvery-white, fern-like leaves. It is only half-hardy in exposed positions in temperate regions.

Zonal pelargoniums usually have attractive horseshoe patterning on their rounded leaves. The flowers, which last from early summer to autumn, come in white, pink, orange and red. Young plants and dwarf forms are ideal for window boxes. These upright, branching shrubs are tender. They are varieties of *Pelargonium × hortorum*. Ivy-leaved geraniums (forms of *P. peltatum*) are also attractive, with trailing stems often 90cm (3ft) long and with mid-green, fleshy leaves. They have the bonus of flowers throughout summer and into autumn, mainly mauve, pink and white. More plants with attractive foliage are discussed on pages 28 and 29.

Geranium 'Emma Smith' also known as 'Caroline Schmidt'

Tradescantia 'Fluminensis'

Pelargonium 'L'Elegante'

FOLIAGE EFFECTS

✳ Greyish plants like *Helichrysum petiolare* play a useful part in different colour schemes. When reds and blues are combined with white, grey will 'cool' the impact of the strong hues. Its neutral tones make the visual leap to palest white less dazzling.

✳ A background of grey foliage will bring out the best in pastel pinks, mauves and misty blues, and will delicately harmonize colour schemes.

✳ Golden foliage tones – and yellow variegation – have affinities with yellow flowers and mid-green leaves. Their presence intensifies the richness of deep blues and violets.

SUMMER FLOWERS AND FOLIAGE

Summer displays in window boxes can be enhanced by selecting plants to suit their backgrounds (and the finish of the window box itself). White, for example, accentuates the impact of yellow, gold, orange, red and dark-blue flowers, as well as of green and brightly coloured foliage. Dark backgrounds highlight white and yellow flowers. Red-brick walls have warm tones that create superb backgrounds for the contrast of white, soft blue, silver and lemon flowers. They also make a good foil for silvery leaves. These soft colours would blend in to the muted tones of grey walls, so for emphasis choose red, pink, deep-blue and deep purple-flowers.

FOLIAGE PLANTS

In addition to those plants discussed on pages 26 and 27 there are others to consider.

Widely known as moneywort and creeping Jenny, *Lysimachia nummularia* is famed for its trailing stems and golden-yellow flowers during early and mid-summer. There is also a yellow-leaved form known as 'Aurea' which adds brightness to window boxes throughout summer. This also has the virtue of being less vigorous than its all-green relative.

The flame nettle or painted nettle (*Coleus blumei*) is well known as a houseplant in temperate countries, but in warm, wind-sheltered positions outdoors it also creates a magnificent display of brightly coloured leaves during summer. Most varieties are bushy and upright, but some trail and are ideal for the front or side of a window box. Trailing types include 'Scarlet Poncho' and 'Molten Lava'. Both of these are also ideal for planting in hanging baskets. The emerald fern (*Asparagus densiflorus* 'Sprengeri') has long, wiry, arching, cascading stems packed with green, needle-like leaves. It is an ideal companion for white-flowered plants. A combination of white and green is ideal for creating a restful and soothing ambience.

ABOVE Bright colours are usually best for a white wall. Petunias, lobelias and geraniums (pelargoniums) have become classic window box plants and here a careful selection of bluish-reds and reddish-blues, together with a good sprinkling of white and green, ensures that the effect is colourful without being strident.

ABOVE The foliage in this window box forms the perfect background to the brightly coloured flowers, creating a naturally cascading display of summer flowers and foliage.

SCENTED SUMMER DISPLAYS

Few window boxes are as captivating as those packed with fragrant plants:

* Plant sweet alyssum (*Lobularia maritima*, earlier known as *Alyssum maritimum*) with its fragrance of new-mown hay at one corner, and cool, sweetly scented pansies at the other. Between them use short varieties of the fragrant flowering tobacco plant (*Nicotiana alata*) and deep-purple heliotrope (*Heliotropium* × *hybridum*), which is claimed by many gardeners to smell of cherry pie.

The variegated ground ivy (*Glechoma hederacea* 'Variegata') is good for positioning at the sides of a window box and at least 1.2m (4ft) above the ground. It creates long stems and a mass of mid-green, kidney-shaped leaves with white markings. During late spring and early summer it has the bonus of small lilac-blue flowers. It is a useful trailing plant as it trails without first creating a dome of foliage, which might obscure attractive flowers immediately behind it. Sometimes this unassuming but very worthy foliage plant is sold under its earlier and well-established name *Nepeta hederacea* 'Variegata'.

RIGHT Standing potted plants on shelves is a type of gardening which originated in France. It was used both indoors and on courtyard and house walls. Both single and mixed colour themes can be used. Three colours combined in this way is stunningly effective. Positioning plants on shelves like this was very popular in Victorian times.

ABOVE An old lead water cistern provides an ideal home for plants, enabling them to be displayed at waist height. Plants in pots can be positioned around the base of the containers. Some of those used here, such as the hostas, can be left outdoors all year, while cacti need the comfort of a frost-free greenhouse during winter.

ABOVE Few flowering plants for window boxes and troughs have such a bright and dramatic impact as the tuberous-rooted *Begonia* x *tuberhybrida*. Throughout summer it bears large, rose-like, single or double flowers in a wide colour range including yellow, pink, red and white.

TROUGHS IN SUMMER

With their rectangular shape, troughs present planting challenges similar to those offered by window boxes. Their siting is what is different, and affects the angle at which they are viewed: some troughs stand at ground level, some are raised on legs, and others are set on or against walls.

Troughs raised on walls or legs offer an opportunity to use trailing plants, which are best seen from the sides. Conversely, where troughs are mainly seen from above, choose plants with bright faces that peer upwards. For troughs at ground level, low-growing herbaceous perennials create attractive features. These plants survive from season to season and need be removed only when congested. Split them up and replant young pieces from around the outside of the clump. Discard old, central parts.

Most troughs have a face side from which they are mainly viewed, but troughs on the tops of low walls may be viewed from both sides. Always ensure that the most noticeable sides are well-clothed with plants; if bare – especially during mid-summer, when plants should be drenching troughs in colour – they look unattractive and smack of neglect.

SUITABLE PLANTS

These are very much the same as those used in window boxes, but choose the longer trailing types only where a trough is raised above the ground.

In addition to the summer-flowering bedding plants and relatively small culinary herbs, low-growing herbaceous perennials furnish troughs with colour and texture from early summer to autumn. Plants to consider include the compact *Polygonum affine* 'Donald Lowndes', which forms a mat of bright-green leaves when young. During early summer it reveals rosy-red flower spikes. Heucheras, often known as coral bells and alumroot, are superb, but use low-growing varieties like 'Pewter Moon',

LEFT Home-made troughs formed of ordinary bricks cemented to a concrete base and mounted on four piers create long-term houses for plants. Medleys of low-growing herbaceous perennials and summer-flowering bedding plants create inexpensive displays.

ABOVE As long as a trough is raised in height it can be planted with trailing annuals for a summer display. Upright salvias and geraniums (pelargoniums) can be offset by a cascade of petunias, busy Lizzies and lobelia.

with leaves like marbled pewter above and deep maroon on the underside. Heuchera 'Snowstorm' has leaves variegated with creamy-white.

Low-growing plantain lilies or hostas (once known as funkias) are ideal in troughs where the compost can be kept moist. They are not so tolerant of dry soil as heucheras and are best positioned in light shade. Increasingly, small varieties of hostas are available.

The spiky, silver-blue grass *Festuca glauca* 'Blue Glow' tolerates dry soil; it forms attractive mounds. The variety 'Sea Urchin' has blue-green

leaves that introduce some tonal interest.

Epimediums, widely known as barrenwort, also survive in dry soil; most are up to 30cm (12in) high and therefore do not become too large. They have attractive leaves which, with some species, reveal attractive colours in autumn. They also have clusters of flowers during late spring and into early summer.

If regular watering throughout summer is a problem, herbaceous plants that survive dry soils are the plants to seek.

BELOW Begonias drench troughs and window boxes in colour throughout summer. Normally grown as houseplants in temperate areas they can be put outside in troughs on a warm, sheltered patio.

BELOW Dwarf nasturtiums are superb for brightening troughs and window boxes. As well as creating a mass of flowers during summer, some varieties have leaves that are marbled and striped with cream.

BELOW Troughs constructed of simulated stone blocks have a semi-formal appearance and are ideal for using in modern settings, perhaps amid brightly coloured paving slabs.

Peppermint-scented geranium

Fuchsia 'Brutus'

Geranium 'Gala' and 'Challenge' varieties

Begonia 'Happy Choice'

Fuchsia 'Rose Winston'

Petunia 'Surfina'

Fuchsia 'Rose Winston'

Tagetes 'Boy O Boy Mixed'

EVERGREENS IN WINTER WINDOW BOXES

Miniature conifers and evergreen shrubs create interest in window boxes throughout winter. You can exploit the contrasting forms of these plants as well as their varying leaf textures and colours. Many of these plants, such as some of the miniature conifers, can be left in a window box for several years before they outgrow their space. Others, such as variegated forms of *Euonymus fortunei* and heathers, become too large after just a few years and are then removed and put into a garden to grow to their natural size.

By buying small plants it is possible to have an attractive display of foliage in your window boxes every winter. And these plants are excellent value as they create colour over a long period, and not only in winter.

EVERGREEN FOLIAGE
The choice of plants with attractive foliage is remarkably wide and in addition to the miniature and dwarf conifers featured on the opposite page and trailing types below, includes many small shrubs. Small variegated shrubs create colour throughout the year and are especially useful in winter. *Hebe × franciscana* 'Variegata' is

not fully hardy and therefore best reserved for less exposed positions. Its rounded, rich-green leaves have cream edges, with the bonus of mauve-blue flowers in summer.
Hebe pinguifolia 'Pagei' (also known as *H.* 'Pagei') is diminutive, with small, glaucous leaves. In late spring and early summer it bears spikes of white flowers. When

small, *Hebe × andersonii* 'Variegata' can be used in a winter display in a window box, but eventually it grows 75–90cm (2½–3ft) high and has to be moved to a tub or large pot. Its green and cream leaves are very attractive. Restrict it to sheltered areas.

There are several varieties of *Euonymus fortunei* with attractively variegated leaves.

RIGHT There are many miniature and slow-growing conifers and small shrubs, including trailing varieties, that can be used in window boxes and troughs during winter. Here small conifers are mixed with dwarf hebes, variegated euonymus and small-leaved ivies.

ABOVE A small conifer with yellow foliage combined with a medley of pansies is an easy way to brighten a trough. There are both summer- and winter-flowering pansies in many colours and they all cohabit well with bright-leaved conifers.

TRAILING PLANTS

These are essential for softening the edges of window boxes and linking plants with the container.

＊ Small-leaved forms of *Hedera helix* are the most popular trailing plants. These ivies are hardy, and varieties in mixtures of green and white or green and yellow soon capture attention. Additionally, they are inexpensive to buy and can be easily increased by either taking cuttings or layering a few stems at any time during summer.

＊ *Vinca minor* 'Variegata', the variegated lesser periwinkle, has trailing, sprawling stems clad with green and creamy-white evergreen leaves. When it eventually becomes invasive, move it to the garden and plant a younger specimen grown from a cutting. There are several other forms of vinca with attractively variegated leaves.

These include: 'Emerald Gaiety' (creamy-white and green), 'Emerald 'n' Gold' (green and gold, with pink tinges) and 'Harlequin' (white and green). Eventually these become too large, but while small they are ideal for window boxes. *Euonymus japonicus* 'Microphyllus Variegatus' has small green leaves that reveal white edges. The form *E. j.* 'Microphyllus Pulchellus' (also known as 'Microphyllus

Aureus') has small leaves with golden variegations.

The small-leaved edging box (*Buxus sempervirens* 'Suffruticosa') can also be used when young. It has small, shiny, dark-green leaves that form a superb background for growing variegated trailing plants. Several varieties of heather (*Calluna vulgaris*) have coloured foliage; choose small plants and later transplant them into a garden.

SMALL CONIFERS

Miniature and slow-growing conifers add valuable height to displays in window boxes. There are many exceptionally attractive conifers to choose from, including:

* *Chamaecyparis lawsoniana* 'Ellwoodii' is slow growing and forms a dark-green columnar shape. For a golden colour choose 'Ellwood's Pillar'.

* *Chamaecyparis pisifera* 'Boulevard' is slow growing and forms a cone shape with intense silver-blue foliage.

* *Juniperus communis* 'Compressa' is dwarf and compact, with dark-green, silver-backed, needle-like leaves. This is a miniature form of the Irish juniper and widely grown in containers.

* *Thuja orientalis* 'Aurea Nana' is compact and bun-shaped, with golden foliage.

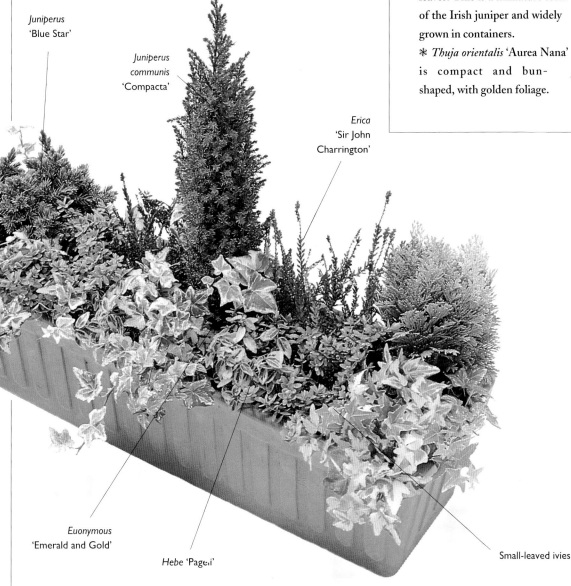

Juniperus 'Blue Star'

Juniperus communis 'Compacta'

Erica 'Sir John Charrington'

Euonymous 'Emerald and Gold'

Hebe 'Pagei'

Small-leaved ivies

Small conifers in pots help to brighten the long winter months. After heavy falls of snow, quickly dust it off before the plant's shape is damaged. However, a light covering often enhances their appearance.

WINTER DISPLAYS IN WINDOW BOXES

Shrubby plants that bear berries widen the range of flower and leaf colour for the window box in winter. Although a few may eventually grow too large they can, for a few years, create a magnificent display. Indeed, the cycle of regularly introducing young plants to window boxes – or other containers – and later transferring the mature specimen to a garden is a mainstay of winter displays. Even plants that eventually become 1.8m (6ft) or more high and wide in gardens can be used for a season or two. An example of this is the spotted laurel *Aucuba japonica* 'Variegata' (also known as *A. j.* 'Maculata').

WINTER FLOWERS

Skimmias are hardy, evergreen shrubs mainly grown in gardens, but when young some are ideal for winter displays in windowboxes. *Skimmia japonica* 'Rubella' produces clusters of bright-red flower buds throughout winter, which open to white in spring and reveal yellow anthers. This is a male form and therefore does not produce berries.

Some heathers are grown for their coloured foliage, which is especially prized in winter displays, while others have flowers throughout much of winter. Some varieties of common heather (*Calluna vulgaris*) have flowers up to early winter, while the spring or snow heather (*Erica herbacea*, also known as *E. carnea*) has flowers from late autumn to late spring.

Erica 'Springwood White'

Erica 'Springwood Park'

Euonymous 'Emerald and Gold'

Small-leaved ivies

LEFT *Erica* × *darleyensis*, a hybrid between *E. herbacea* (earlier known as *E. carnea*) and *E. mediterranea*, develops white, pink or purple flowers from mid-winter until late spring. There are several varieties, including 'Darley Dale' (shown here) with pale-pink flowers.

ABOVE Window boxes and troughs packed with dwarf, variegated evergreen shrubs and trailing plants, and small conifers, create a magnificent display. Winter-flowering ericas can also be put in the display. There are many varieties of *Erica herbacea* (earlier known as *E. carnea*) to choose from, in colours including carmine-red, pink, rosy-red and white. There are also varieties with coloured foliage, such as 'Aurea' which has golden leaves and deep-pink flowers that fade to white.

WINTER-FLOWERING BULBS

Several small bulbs burst into flower between mid-winter and spring and look especially good when grouped among foliage plants. The bulbs can be left in the same position for several years.

These early-flowering bulbs include the winter aconite (*Eranthis hyemalis*), with yellow flowers during late winter and early spring, while snowdrops (*Galanthus nivalis*) come into flower during mid-winter.

Two charming early-flowerers are the bright-yellow *Iris danfordiae*, and *I. reticulata*, which has deep-blue flowers with golden-yellow blazes on the lower petals. Avoid using these miniature bulbs in positions in strong sunlight and where cold winds constantly blow them. Diffused light suits them.

RIGHT *Hebe x andersonii* 'Variegata' is a slightly tender evergreen shrub that is ideal for planting in a trough or window box in a sheltered corner, away from cold winds. The mid-green and cream variegated leaves appear throughout the year, while from mid-summer to autumn lavender flowers appear in spikes up to 13cm (5in) long.

BELOW The winter cherry (*Solanum capsicastrum*) forms a half-hardy evergreen shrub and is often grown as a houseplant in temperate regions. But in sheltered areas it is ideal for displaying in a window box or trough. During winter it creates a mass of marble-like, dark-green fruits that gradually change to yellow, then scarlet.

SCENTED WINTER DISPLAYS

The foliage of some miniature conifers has an intriguing aromatic quality when bruised. Interplant these conifers with small bulbs such as the honey-scented *Iris danfordiae* or violet-scented *I. reticulata* for a display that both looks and smells delightful.

* *Chamaecyparis lawsoniana* 'Ellwoodii' (resin and parsley).
* *Chamaecyparis pisifera* 'Boulevard' (resinous bouquet).
* *Juniperus communis* 'Compressa' (apple-scented).

BERRIES FOR WINTER

Several shrubs produce attractive berries in autumn and winter. Here are two, but choose small plants.

* *Cotoneaster microphyllus thymifolius* has a creeping nature, with small, narrow leaves and white flowers in early summer. In autumn and early winter these are followed by scarlet berries.

* *Gaultheria procumbens* (partridge berry/winter green) is evergreen, with creeping stems and bright-red, round berries in winter.

WINTER DISPLAYS IN TROUGHS

Most plants suitable for winter window box displays also suit troughs. However, troughs are often set at lower levels and viewed from above, and for these a simple approach is best, choosing bright flowers with upward-looking faces. Two or three miniature conifers amid a sea of small winter-flowering bulbs produces a spectactular display. For an even simpler arrangement, choose several miniature conifers with contrasting shapes and colours and surround them with pea-shingle. This stark, rather abstract display suits a modernistic setting perfectly, but where the aura is more old-fashioned or informal, a more casual and freer design with small bulbs softened by a few trailing and sprawling evergreens is in keeping.

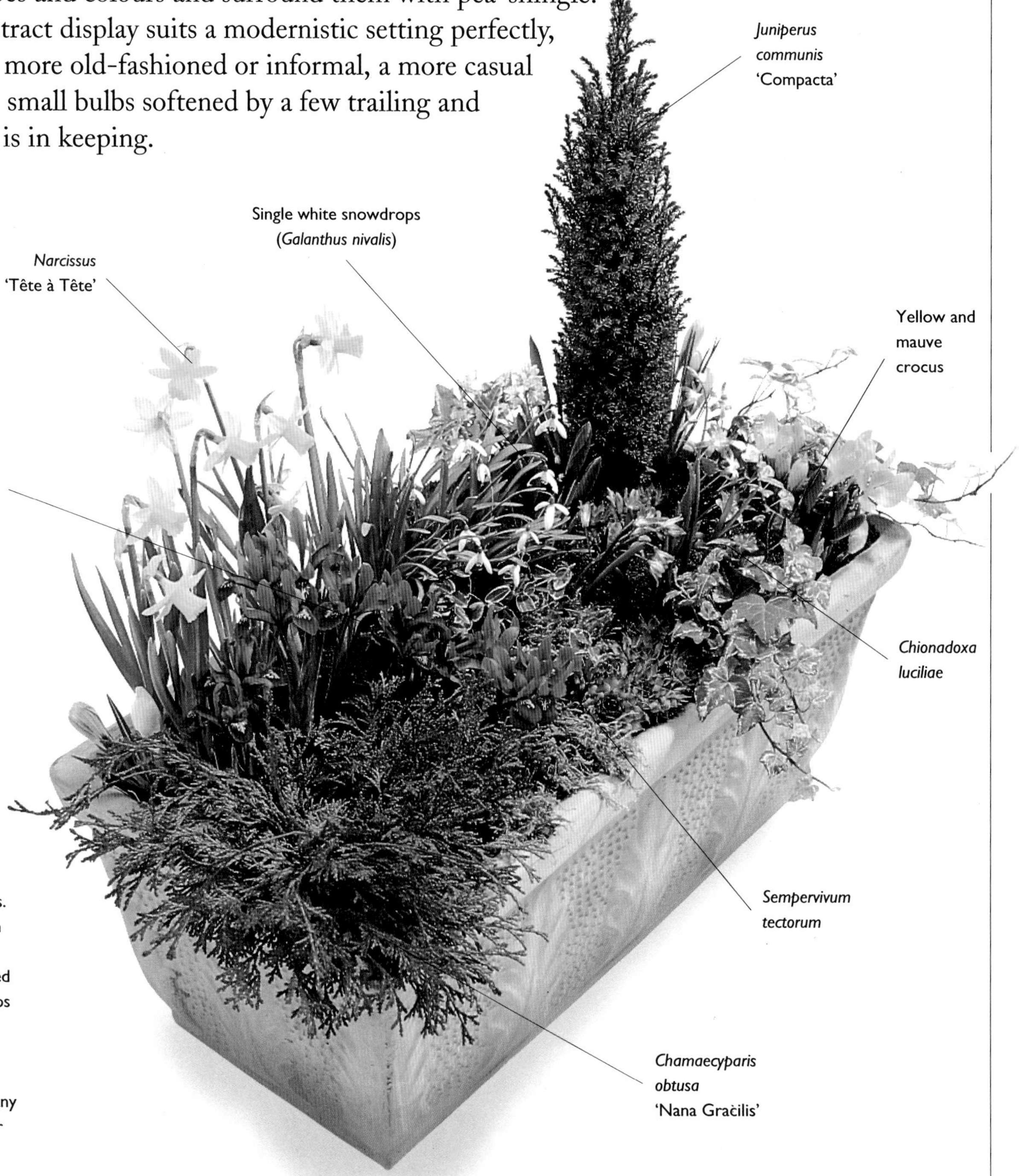

Juniperus communis 'Compacta'

Single white snowdrops
(*Galanthus nivalis*)

Narcissus 'Tête à Tête'

Yellow and mauve crocus

Iris reticulata

Chionadoxa luciliae

RIGHT Troughs and window boxes planted with miniature conifers, dwarf shrubs and variegated trailing plants can be further brightened by dwarf late winter- and spring-flowering bulbs. These are planted in the display in autumn and can be left in position until the clumps become congested and need to be divided. Snowdrops (*Galanthus*), crocuses, dwarf irises and miniature daffodils are ideal companions for evergreens and other more permanent plants. Many of these bulbs are also suitable for inclusion in spring displays.

Sempervivum tectorum

Chamaecyparis obtusa 'Nana Gracilis'

POSITIONING WINTER DISPLAYS

Troughs with summer displays can thrive in exposed positions, perhaps on top of a low wall. But winter displays may need protection, especially in cold and exposed gardens. Also, avoid positions where strong, early morning sun shines directly on relatively soft leaves thickly covered with frost. Conifers are hardier and are not damaged by rapidly thawing frost. For full enjoyment, position them where they can be easily seen, perhaps near a door or at least where they can be viewed and admired from a window.

ABOVE Even the smallest trough can be brightened in winter by the introduction of a few small conifers. And once planted it creates a feature for many years; when too large, replant the conifers into a garden.

CREATING INTERESTING TROUGHS

In summer, trailing summer-flowering bedding plants create such a wealth of colour that the sides of a trough – or a window box – are not readily noticed. In winter and spring it is a different matter, as the box itself is more exposed.

To enliven plain wooden troughs, glue or nail strips of wood, about 12mm (½in) thick and 18–25mm (¾–1in) wide to the sides.

Alternatively, create a rustic look by securing bark or thin log sections to them. This is especially effective when the winter display is formed of miniature conifers and winter-flowering heathers with colourful foliage.

Do not paint wooden troughs intended for winter-flowering displays in bright, pure hues such as yellow or blue. This will detract attention from the plants, which in winter have a more subdued appearance than during summer months.

Juniperus communis 'Compacta'

Euonymous 'Emerald and Gold'

Chamaecyparis pisafera 'Filifera Aurea'

Small-leaved ivies

ABOVE In winter, wooden troughs harmonize well with foliage plants such as miniature conifers and trailing evergreens. Brightly coloured troughs are more suited to flowering plants in summer.

FLORIFEROUS CINERARIAS

Cinerarias (*Senecio × hybridus*, sometimes known as *Cineraria × hybrida*, among other names) are popular houseplants. Produced commercially in greenhouses, they flower from mid-winter to early summer. In warm and sheltered positions they can also be put into window boxes and troughs – outdoors, or in a porch. Their large, dome-shaped heads packed with bright daisy-like flowers in a spectrum that includes white, pink, red, lavender-blue and mauve banish winter gloom with cheering splashes of intense colour.

Before putting a cineraria outside, slowly acclimatize it to cool conditions. Should the weather be exceptionally cold, defer putting plants outside until the temperature rises. Preferably position the trough against a warm, sunny wall.

SPRING DISPLAYS IN WINDOW BOXES

Spring-flowering displays in window boxes are prepared in autumn, when bulbs and biennials such as wallflowers and daisies are planted. In late winter or early spring – as soon as the plants are creating a colourful display – the box holding the winter display is removed and the spring one put in its place. Take care not to unduly disturb the plants.

Many spring displays are entirely formed from bulbs. Others use bulbs in combination with biennials or miniature conifers, which create a greater sense of permanence to the display. Where window boxes are planted with fragrant flowers, it is essential to position them against a warm, sheltered wall. Sash-type windows are better than casements for these displays, as the bouquet filters more easily into rooms from flowers above sill level.

SCENTED SPRING WINDOW BOXES

The miniature conifers with aromatic foliage listed on page 35 form an attractive basis for spring displays that feature scented flowers. Bulbs are the epitome of spring and – as well as the floriferous hyacinths – many of the smaller ones that are suitable for window boxes have the bonus of fragrance. Some of these bulbs begin flowering in late winter and continue well into spring. Always position window boxes with scented bulbs in a sheltered position, where their fragrance is not quickly dissipated. Scented bulbs to consider include:
* *Crocus chrysanthus*: Sweet, from late winter to spring.
* *Hyacinthus orientalis* varieties: Sweet, from spring to early summer. Several colours.
* *Iris danfordiae*: Honey-like scent, from mid-winter to early spring.
* *Iris reticulata*: Captivating violet bouquet, from late winter to early spring.

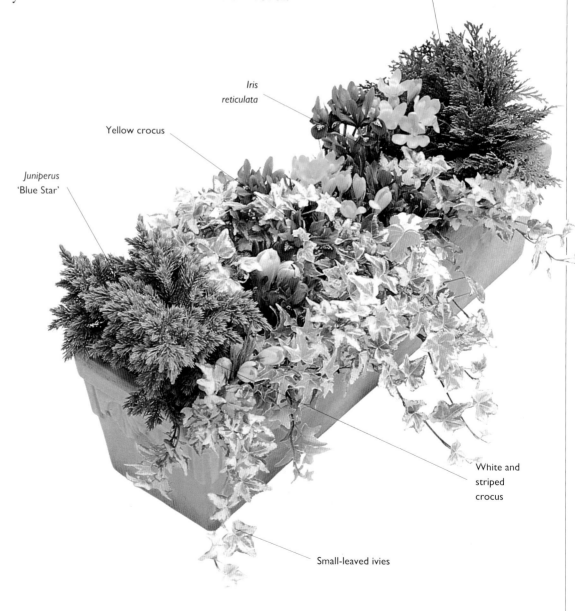

Chamaecyparis 'Minima'

Iris reticulata

Yellow crocus

Juniperus 'Blue Star'

White and striped crocus

Small-leaved ivies

COLOUR THEMES FOR SPRING

✳ For simple impact, pack the window box with bright-yellow narcissi, chosen to be in scale with your container.

✳ Underplant red *Tulipa fosteriana* or *T. greigii* with a sea of blue forget-me-nots. Include a few grape hyacinths for darker accents and texture. Edge the box with double daisies.

✳ For an alternative version of the reds-white-and-blues theme, combine a range of hyacinths with the daisies and forget-me-nots.

✳ Mix wallflowers in tapestry colours, or choose reds and yellows to accompany tulips and daffodils.

✳ For sheer brightness intersperse multicoloured polyanthus with low-growing trumpet daffodils.

✳ For simple two-colour contrast, plant yellow polyanthus in a sea of blue grape hyacinths.

BIENNIALS FOR SPRING

As a complement to the range of bulbs, there are several superb biennials that, inexpensively, create colourful displays. Plants can be easily raised by sowing seed outdoors in a seedbed during late spring or early summer, thinning out the seedlings when large enough to handle and planting them into window boxes in autumn. Biennials include:

• Daisies (*Bellis perennis*) create a feast of white-petalled flowers with yellow centres from spring onwards. The plants make an attractive edging. The range of varieties and colours is wide and includes red, pink and carmine, some with double flowers.

• Wallflowers (*Cheiranthus cheiri*) are raised in the same way as daisies and flower during spring and early summer. Their scent is a special bonus. Dwarf varieties are best in containers, especially in exposed areas, and are available in many rich, glowing shades including red, yellow, orange, white and pink.

• Forget-me-nots (*Myosotis sylvatica*) are popular, with lightly fragrant, misty- or clear-blue flowers in spring and early summer. Raise new plants from seed, in the same way as for daisies. Choose low-growing varieties, preferably 15–20cm (6–8in) high. Containers only planted with forget-me-nots are superb.

ABOVE The common snowdrop (*Galanthus nivalis*) is a hardy bulb that is ideal for planting in containers where it creates a display of white flowers with green markings during late winter and into early spring.

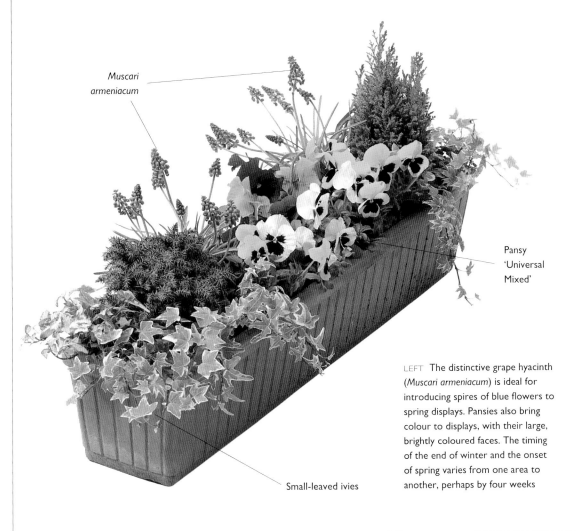

Muscari armeniacum

Pansy 'Universal Mixed'

Small-leaved ivies

LEFT The distinctive grape hyacinth (*Muscari armeniacum*) is ideal for introducing spires of blue flowers to spring displays. Pansies also bring colour to displays, with their large, brightly coloured faces. The timing of the end of winter and the onset of spring varies from one area to another, perhaps by four weeks within a distance of a few hundred miles. In cold areas, late winter-flowering bulbs may still be creating a spectacular display, while in slightly warmer areas these may have finished their show to be replaced by spring-flowering bulbs and biennials (see above for a range of these reliably flowering plants).

CO-ORDINATING SPRING DISPLAYS

Window boxes are not always the only containers in the picture. When there are nearby urns and tubs to be planted, it is a good idea to co-ordinate the flowers in the various containers, just as you match or link the contents of your different window boxes. Where troughs, tubs or pots are positioned near window boxes, choose taller varieties of trumpet daffodils for the containers on the ground and smaller ones for the window boxes. Unify them with the same companion plants – wallflowers, forget-me-nots, daisies, and so on. White urns densely planted with blue grape hyacinths and yellow daffodils look superb near white window boxes with matching planting.

ABOVE Pink and red hyacinths are prevented from becoming excessively dominant by positioning them against a light-grey background. They can make a stronger impact when placed against a white wall.

CONSIDERING BACKGROUNDS

Creating a spring display which makes a statement when set against its background is no more expensive than randomly planting a window box.

* For white backgrounds choose contrasting flowers such as blue forget-me-nots, golden or red wallflowers, pink daisies, yellow *Crocus chrysanthus*, blue or red hyacinths and yellow daffodils. To subdue the contrast slightly and link the planting with its backdrop, intersperse a few white flowers.

* For displays that shine out against dark backgrounds, select plants such as white, cream or yellow hyacinths, yellow *Crocus chrysanthus*, yellow-variegated ivies, yellow polyanthus, white tulips and yellow daffodils.

* For contrast against red-brick walls, choose light-blue forget-me-nots, white hyacinths, bronze and cream wallflowers, blue grape hyacinths, yellow-variegated ivies, yellow polyanthus and white tulips.

* For rich contrast with grey stone walls select red wallflowers, deep-blue forget-me-nots, pink tulips and pink or blue hyacinths.

OPPOSITE On a warm, wind-sheltered patio, slightly tender plants such as the variegated century plant can be grown in an urn on a pedestal or at ground level. Here, this succulent forms part of a superb display in late spring and early summer with a white wisteria and the young flowers of French lavender (*Lavandula stoechas*). The dull, creamy-white walls admirably highlight all of these plants.

MIXING AND MATCHING

For a simple but effective spring medley, combine wallflowers (*Cheiranthus cheiri*), the waterlily tulip (*Tulipa kaufmanniana*) and the short-stemmed varieties of golden-yellow, trumpet daffodils.

RIGHT Blue-flowered irises, such as this deep-blue *Iris reticulata*, have their colouring softened or intensified depending on the colour of the background against which they are set. Give them a white background to create a dramatic feature.

OPPOSITE, BELOW Pots of white hyacinths stand out against a dark background. This is essential if the flowers are not to be lost among other larger and more dominantly coloured plants.

SPRING DISPLAYS IN TROUGHS

Large or small, chunky or finely proportioned troughs bring spring to your doorstep in a wide variety of moods. Yellow is the colour that best symbolizes spring. It is superb on its own. Combined with whites and creams, with perhaps a hint of blue, its effect is demure and delicate. Mixed with splashes of other dominant colours, it adds zest to the most vibrant of spring displays.

Daffodils in a whole gamut of sizes are spring's main heralds. Trumpet daffodils combine well in larger troughs with polyanthus and grape hyacinths, while diminutive ones, such as the hoop-petticoat narcissus (*Narcissus bulbocodium*) and *N. cyclamineus* with its swept back petals and small, tubular trumpet, look charming beside miniature conifers, which add a note of permanency as well as wind protection.

In winter, troughs are often brought near to windows and doors so that they can be easily seen from indoors. In spring you can move them to the far side of a patio so that they become areas of focus, especially when filled with bright colours. But keep troughs full of small-scale or scented flowers near to the house, where they can be enjoyed at close quarters, perhaps near a door or window.

SIMPLE COMBINATIONS
Some spring-flowering troughs can be packed with five or more different types of plants that create combinations of colour and form, but attractive displays can be created from just two or three of them:
* For a green, white and cream mixture that flowers during late winter and into spring plant the Lenten rose (*Helleborus orientalis*), an evergreen w-shaped cream flower during late winter and early spring. There are also

Grape hyacinths (*Muscari armeniacum*) form a superb partnership with polyanthus. Here, the blue flowers of the grape hyacinths harmonize with pink and red polyanthus. This simple display harmonizes again with the terracotta trough. These plants can be highlighted by planting them in a white container.

THE PANSY FACTOR

Pansies are superb in winter as well as summer, and if you select early-flowering varieties it is possible to have flowers throughout spring, in the colour of your choice. Sow seeds in a moisture-retentive, cool, lightly shaded seed-bed in early to mid-summer and plant in containers in autumn.

---

forms with pink, white, crimson or purple flowers. It grows 45–50cm (18–20in) high in a container and can be planted with varieties of waterlily tulips. Their flowers mostly have two colours; the white and cream varieties harmonize best with the hellebore. *Helleborus × sternii*, is an alternative hellebore.

For a simple yet scented display, plant hyacinths among a mixture of polyanthus and auriculas. The upright, stiff and soldier-like hyacinths create a shape contrast with the circular-faced auriculas and polyanthus. Use warm but not strongly coloured hyacinths, such as rich, deep pink or light orange.

The auriculas have less tightly bunched heads than the polyanthus and their old-fashioned character brings a tinge of nostalgia to the display. All of these flowers are scented, so position the display near a window where a light draught will help to disperse the scent. Protect the display from winds.

Tulipa
'Prince of Austria'

LEFT A rustic trough creates an ideal setting for a medley of biennial plants and bulbs. At the front of the display are double-flowered pink daisies (*Bellis perennis*), backed by vivid red wallflowers and dark-pink tulips. This sort of display is ideal for placing against a white background.

Wallflower
'Blood Red'

Pink
Bellis Perennis

HANGING BASKETS AND WALL BASKETS

These containers are welcome for bringing garden displays on to a higher plane. Hanging baskets suspended from overhead structures such as beams or projecting roofs, or by means of brackets, can introduce decoration to vertical surfaces. Wall baskets are like large hanging baskets cut in half vertically and secured to a wall. Mangers are similar, but usually larger; formed of flat strips of metal, they also tend to look more robust (*see pages 64 and 65*).

Both hanging baskets and wall baskets are ideal for brightening walls, balconies, verandahs, porches, lobbies and roof gardens. In the garden itself, hanging baskets can be suspended from rustic arches and pergolas before they become clothed in climbing plants, and wall baskets can be attached to fences.

In temperate countries, most baskets are used only for summer-flowering displays; in autumn, the plants are removed and the container stored during winter. However, in porches and lobbies, where plants in hanging baskets can be protected, houseplants can be displayed throughout winter.

VIEWING ANGLES

Hanging baskets are secured to walls at about head or shoulder height, displaying plants that are seen mainly from the side. Cascading and trailing plants are therefore essential. Add a few bushy types in the centre to provide height that will visually balance the basket's width when it is drenched in colourful flowers during mid- and late summer.

Wall baskets and mangers are often fixed only at about waist height, so it is the plants at the top that are mainly seen from close to. When viewed from a distance, the sides become more noticeable. Therefore, pack the top with bushy plants with upward-facing flowers, and plant the sides with trailing types that will completely camouflage the framework and create a magnificent feast of colour.

OPPOSITE AND ABOVE Hanging baskets and wall baskets create a feast of colour at head and waist height. Whatever a garden's size it is possible to fit in at least one of these features. Choose the colours of the flowers to harmonize or contrast with their background.

THE DRIP FACTOR

Most hanging baskets are formed of a wire frame and rely on compost and a plastic liner or sphagnum moss to retain moisture in them. Because these containers need to be watered two or three times a day during summer, they invariably drip afterwards and therefore it is essential not to position wall baskets or groups of plants in pots and tubs directly under them.

Some hanging baskets are formed of a plastic shell with a drip-tray built into the base to prevent water from dripping on plants below them. These baskets are especially useful in porches and lobbies, where repeated moistening might damage a wooden floor or stain floor tiles. They are also useful on balconies, which are often crowded with pots of plants.

DESIGNING WITH HANGING BASKETS

Hanging baskets are extremely versatile containers. They are decorative in their own right; they can be used to highlight aspects of architecture – such as to emphasize doorways – or deployed to cloak unappealing items like drainpipes. As well as considering colour effects, look at the whole picture when choosing where to place your baskets. Avoid just dotting them about: they make a much stronger impact if they relate to the position of doors and windows, enhancing symmetry or balancing existing features.

Apart from displaying hanging baskets on buildings, you can suspend them from free standing supports such as old-fashioned street lamp-posts with arms. Installed in front gardens, these lamp standards provide illumination as well as being decorative. Because hanging baskets displayed in this way are exposed to drying winds, there is a risk of the compost becoming excessively dry. Adding vermiculite or perlite to the compost assists in the retention of moisture, while using foliage plants that are able to survive dry conditions is another. Many grey- and silver-leaved plants are naturally drought-tolerant; the cascading silver-leaved *Helichrysum petiolare* is an example. But never expect it to thrive in totally dry compost. Regular feeding and watering produces better plants.

ABOVE This floor-standing hanging basket creates a stunning ball of brightly coloured flowers and foliage and would enhance a patio or garden.

USING WALL BASKETS

Wall baskets and mangers are ideal for securing to walls below windows, as well as between windows. Combine them with hanging baskets to create colourful features on long, bare walls – you could use a hanging basket on either side of a wall basket, for example, or vice versa. As well as choosing flower and foliage colours that look good against the wall, unify the feature by choosing two slightly different but related colour themes, one for the two flanking baskets and the other for the central basket.

Wall baskets are ideal for introducing colour to roof gardens and are much more secure than hanging baskets. Additionally, because they hold more compost than hanging baskets, the plants are at less risk during dry weather.

ARCHITECTURAL ACCENTS

Because every house has walls, every garden offers a range of opportunities to use hanging baskets, whether on a patio, terrace or verandah, in a courtyard or beside doors or windows.

* Position matching hanging baskets on either side of a front door, so that cascading plants slightly cut across the uprights of the frame. This will make the door area appear larger and more distinguished. Ensure, however, that the baskets cannot be knocked and that water does not drip on other plants or make a pathway slippery.

* Windows can be treated in the same way as the front door, with foliage and flowers bisecting the framework on the outer edges. If the window also has a window box, ensure that water from the hanging basket does not drip on it.

* Where a large expanse of bare wall stretches between two windows, brighten the area by securing a hanging basket halfway along it. Where a house has three equally spaced windows, use two hanging baskets for symmetry.

* Windows that have frosted glass – perhaps a bathroom – often look bleak and unappealing. If they are on the side of the house, position a

hanging basket so that it obliquely blocks the view from the front.

* Verandahs can often be swathed in climbers, but they also look superb with hanging baskets suspended from above. As part or all of the basket is under cover, regular watering is essential, but take care to prevent drips.

* Large areas of wall benefit from a few well-placed baskets. Take the colour of the wall into account when selecting flower colours. More ideas for co-ordinating plants with their backgrounds are given on pages 64 and 65.

* Carports are stark and functional and in need of plants to brighten them. Position a couple of hanging baskets on either side of the front. Include white flowers and silver-leaved plants, as they show up well at night.

* Roof gardens, especially, benefit from a little colour at head height, but always ensure that the hanging basket is not positioned in a particularly blustery and wind-swept position.

* Balconies also benefit from hanging baskets, but ensure strong wind cannot damage the plants and that water does not drip on balconies or people below. Use plastic baskets with drip-trays built into their base.

* When positioning a hanging basket against a long wall, do not secure it right at the end where it could be exposed to wind and is likely to be knocked by people walking around the corner.

* Summer-houses – especially those with verandahs and widely overhanging eaves – can be brightened by a couple of hanging baskets. Ensure that the compost is kept moist.

ABOVE Hanging baskets positioned either side of a decorative door or window help to highlight its attractive features. Position the baskets so that they bisect the sides of the door or window; in this way they help to make it look larger.

COMPOSTS, BASKETS AND PLANTING

Success can be more elusive with hanging baskets than any other type of container. Moisture-retentive compost, a large basket and planting the hanging basket as early as possible so that plants are well-established before it is placed in position are a few keys to success. Choosing the compost is discussed on this page, while planting is detailed opposite.

Traditional hanging baskets are formed of a bowl-shaped wire framework, usually coated in white, black or green plastic. Some modern types are formed of plastic, with a drip-tray in their base to prevent excess water dripping on anything beneath them. These are especially useful in lobbies, porches and conservatories and where a floor-covering below might be damaged by excessive moisture.

COMPOST AND ADDITIVES

Proprietary composts are sold specially for use in hanging baskets and wall baskets, where it is essential that the compost is both nutritious and moisture-retentive. A mixture of equal parts peat-based and loam-based compost is ideal. The peat type retains plenty of water, but is difficult to re-moisten when dry; the loam-based compost counteracts this deficiency and provides nutrients over a long period. As an aid to moisture retention, perlite and vermiculite can also be added. Proprietary basket liners assist in water retention.

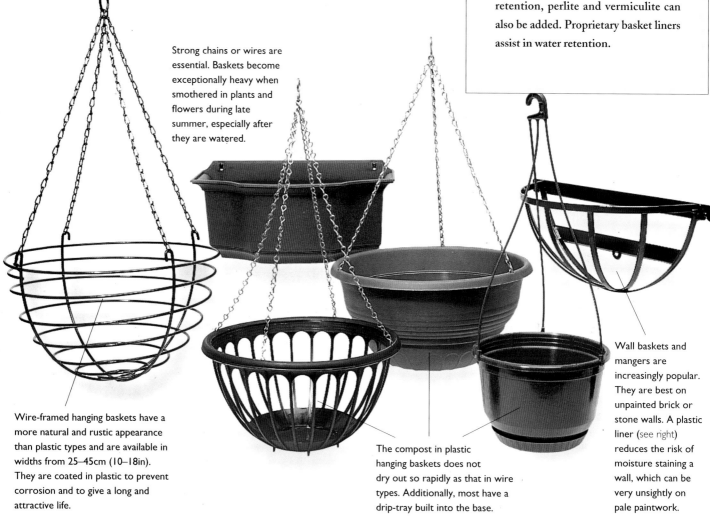

Strong chains or wires are essential. Baskets become exceptionally heavy when smothered in plants and flowers during late summer, especially after they are watered.

Wire-framed hanging baskets have a more natural and rustic appearance than plastic types and are available in widths from 25–45cm (10–18in). They are coated in plastic to prevent corrosion and to give a long and attractive life.

The compost in plastic hanging baskets does not dry out so rapidly as that in wire types. Additionally, most have a drip-tray built into the base.

Wall baskets and mangers are increasingly popular. They are best on unpainted brick or stone walls. A plastic liner (see right) reduces the risk of moisture staining a wall, which can be very unsightly on pale paintwork.

TIMING

Start planting a hanging basket in mid- to late spring in warm areas, but during early summer in cold regions. Planting can be earlier if a greenhouse or conservatory is available to give the plants protection during cold nights in spring, when frost is forecast.

1 Place a wire-framed hanging basket in the top of a large bucket to hold it firm. Then line it with a sheet of black plastic. Use a couple of layers if the plastic is thin. Traditionally, baskets were lined with sphagnum moss, but this can be expensive.

2 Fill the bottom half with compost and lightly firm it with your fingers. Use a sharp, pointed knife to make 5cm (2in) long slits in the plastic around the side. Also, trim off the plastic about 5cm (2in) above the rim of the basket. Later, when full of compost and planting is complete, excess plastic can be further cut back to form a neat outline.

3 Push the roots of trailing and cascading plants through slits in the plastic and spread their roots over the compost. Ensure the plants are evenly spaced. Form a thin layer of compost over them and to within 7.5cm (3in) of the top, then gently firm it.

4 Place a large feature plant, such as a cascading fuchsia, in the centre of the basket. Ensure that the top of this plant's soil-ball is about 12mm (½in) below the rim of the basket. This is to ensure that when planting is complete there is sufficient space at the top to enable the compost to be watered. If the soil-ball of the central plant is too large, remove some compost from the base but do not disturb those plants earlier planted.

To ensure that plants in hanging baskets establish rapidly, make sure their compost is moist by watering it the previous day.

5 Put a ring of small, bushy but cascading plants around the central plant. Position them at a slight angle, facing outwards. Firm compost around them and to within 12mm (½in) of the rim, then use a watering-can and gently but thoroughly water the compost. Spread the water evenly over the surface, so that all the compost is moistened. The surface will settle slightly after a week.

6 If the weather is fine, and no frost is forecast, place the hanging basket outdoors immediately, though not in direct sunshine. If there is any risk of frost, keep the basket in a greenhouse or conservatory at night, placing it outdoors in the day. During this period, keep the compost moist; more water is needed as the plants get bigger and bear flowers. Always ensure that the compost is moist.

LINING WALL BASKETS AND MANGERS

Line wall baskets and mangers with black plastic, ensuring it overlaps the back and front top edges. This prevents compost falling out of the container, conserves moisture and reduces the chance of water running through the manger and directly down a colour-washed wall. Neatly overlap the plastic at the ends. It is easier to cut off excess plastic after compost has been placed in the container.

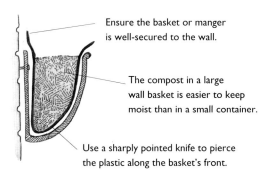

Ensure the basket or manger is well-secured to the wall.

The compost in a large wall basket is easier to keep moist than in a small container.

Use a sharply pointed knife to pierce the plastic along the basket's front. It encourages water to drip from the front, rather than trickling down a wall.

WATERING, FEEDING AND LOOKING AFTER

Plants in hanging baskets soon suffer and create an uninspiring display if irregularly watered and not fed. This especially applies to displays in small hanging baskets as they do not have a large amount of compost to retain moisture.

If a hanging basket is neglected, cut back stems that are severely wilted and will not recover, and immerse the compost in a large bowl of water. Then, remove and place in a lightly shaded position until the plants start to recover.

If plants appear to wilt slightly during early afternoon on exceptionally hot days, yet the compost is moist, this is because they cannot absorb moisture quick enough. In these circumstances, the plants usually recover by late evening.

WATERING

Keeping compost moist in a hanging basket is a regular task throughout summer. Adding materials such as perlite and vermiculite to compost improves its moisture-retaining ability. Also, basket liners assist in water retention.

1 Standing on top of a stool or pair of steps is the most popular way to water hanging baskets, but it is not without its perils. Insecure garden stools and step-ladders on soft surfaces soon cause accidents. Preferably, ask a friend to hold the stool or steps secure. And do not use an excessively large watering-can, as this can upset your balance or severely strain muscles in backs, and arms.

2 A safer way to water the baskets is to use a proprietary lance which can be screwed on the end of a hosepipe. These watering arms are several feet long and enable water to be trickled slowly on the compost. Alternatively, tie the end 1.2m (4ft) of a hosepipe to a bamboo cane and bend over the tip. A piece of wire (perhaps taken from a wire clothes-hanger) can be used to keep the tip bent. When using these watering devices, ensure that strong jets of water do not scatter compost; it may splash over you.

3 Where a hanging basket is displayed high on a wall, the most convenient way to water the compost is to suspend it from a pulley so that it can be lowered. When the basket reaches the ground – and before its base is fully clothed in foliage and flowers – stand it in the top of a large bucket. When it is smothered in plants, tie off the cable when the basket is about 30cm (12in) above the ground. Install new cables each year and regularly check the pulley and its mounting.

4 If a hanging basket is regularly watered, the compost remains evenly moist and able to accept new moisture at each watering. However, when a compost with a high proportion of peat becomes exceptionally dry it is difficult to remoisten quickly and several waterings at frequent intervals over a period of a few days are essential.

A quick way to remoisten the compost is to dunk the basket in a large bowl full of water. However, this is usually only possible when the plants are small. Leave the compost immersed until bubbles cease to rise from it. Then, remove and allow excess water to drain before replacing the basket in its display position.

FEEDING

By the early part of mid-summer, plants in hanging baskets have often absorbed all nutrients in compost. Feeding is then essential.

Adding concentrated liquid or powdered fertilizers to water and applying them every two to three weeks revitalizes plants and extends their flowering season. Always adhere to the manufacturer's instructions.

Houseplants are often fed by adding feeding sticks or pills to the compost. This is a clean and easy method but does tend to encourage roots to mass around them. Therefore, evenly spread them throughout the basket.

PESTS

Whenever plants are massed together it encourages the presence of pests. Greenfly are the main pests and must be controlled before they reach plague proportions. Indeed, spraying plants several times throughout summer with a systemic insecticide (it gets into a plant's sap stream and makes it toxic to insects) is recommended.

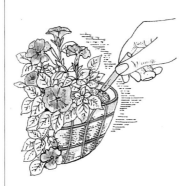

Spraying plants with an insecticide from an environmentally friendly aerosol or through a hand-held spray are popular methods of using chemicals. An alternative way is to insert small sticks impregnated with insect-killing chemicals into the compost, so that roots absorb the chemical and make plants toxic to insects. These are best used in long-term plants grown in lobbies, porches or indoors. After handling pest-killing chemicals, always thoroughly wash your hands in soapy water. And never allow chemicals to splash into eyes.

DEAD-HEADING

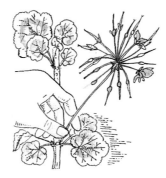

Regularly removing dead flowers encourages the development of further blooms. Additionally, removing dead heads prevents them decaying and encouraging the presence of diseases. Some flowers have a mass of small flowers and these are removed individually by either pulling or twisting them sideways. Some plants, such as pelargoniums, bear flowers at the ends of long stalks. Use a sharp knife or scissors to cut back old flowered stems.

ENCOURAGING BUSHINESS

Tall, lanky plants in hanging baskets are unsightly and do not produce the best display. Some plants naturally have a bushy habit, with each stem creating further sideshoots. But some plants need encouragement by nipping out their growing points while young. Fuchsias when young, for example, benefit from having shoots snapped sideways or pinched off. Try to position the break just above a leaf, so that a short stem is not left – it dies back and decays.

COPING WITH LATE FROSTS

In some years, unexpected late spring or early summer frosts devastate plants in hanging baskets. If these are forecast, spread a couple of layers of newspapers over plants during early evening and remove them the following morning, as soon as the temperature rises.

Wedge them under the chains that suspend the basket, although frosts that occur when skies are cloudless in the early part of the year are not usually accompanied by wind that would disturb the newspaper. Try not to compress or disturb plants unduly.

MIXING FLOWERS AND FOLIAGE

Foliage plants play an important part in hanging baskets. Soon after a basket has been put together, and before flowering plants begin to perform, foliage endows the display with its basic shape and background colouring. Once flowering begins, foliage plants with stiff stems provide a supporting framework through which thin-stemmed half-hardy annuals and even climbers can develop.

Some foliage plants are totally hardy and survive outdoors during winter, while others can be put outside only in summer. Besides these, a few foliage plants which are grown as houseplants in temperate countries are sufficiently hardy to create a display outdoors in warm areas during summer. These plants are also ideal in hanging baskets in porches and lobbies (*see pages 62 and 63*).

TRAILING FOLIAGE

There are several excellent plants with trailing and cascading foliage that clothe the sides of a hanging basket with much needed leaf colour. Choose colours and textures to co-ordinate with the flowers you select from those listed on pages 54 to 61. Among the superb trailing foliage plants detailed here, some are not sufficiently hardy to be left outdoors throughout the year. These are propagated each year so that young plants with bright leaves are available in late spring or early summer.

The liquorice plant, *Helichrysum petiolare* (or *H. petiolatum*) is one of these tender plants. It has stiffish, arching stems and rounded white leaves covered with woolly hairs. It often spreads too widely, but nipping out the growing tips when young encourages it to create a more branched and spreading habit. Indeed, it is better to encourage branching at an early stage than to wait until a few stems become too long and only then nip out their tips. Plants that become lanky and sparse are unsightly.

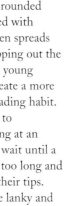

Begonia 'Non Stop'

Asparagus 'Sprengeri'

Pelargonium 'L'Elegante'

BASKETS AGAINST WHITE WALLS

White walls create bright backgrounds which especially highlight yellow, gold and red flowers, together with green foliage plants.

* Use a combination of red geraniums, red and pink zinnias, short varieties of marigolds, and the asparagus fern (*Asparagus densiflorus* 'Sprengeri').

* Another display could be formed from trailing nasturtiums, yellow calceolarias, a dark-red fuchsia, and asparagus fern.

A colour variation on this plant is *H. p.* 'Aureum', also known as 'Limelight'. Its softly golden leaves are more restful on the eye in strong sunlight and blend well with yellow flowers to create a yellow-theme basket.

There is also a grey-leaved form of *Helichrysum petiolare* with much smaller leaves. This is sometimes available as *H. microphyllum*. It is generally more compact, and well-suited to smaller-scale baskets.

Small-leaved ivies (*Hedera helix*) are very hardy and can be left outdoors all year. It is the variegated forms, with yellow and green or white and green leaves, that are mainly put into displays. Occasionally, young and small plants of the larger-leaved *H. canariensis* 'Variegata' are used; the leaves are dark green in the centre and merge through dull silver to creamy-white at the edges.

The well-known creeping Jenny or moneywort (*Lysimachia nummularia*) is a hardy plant grown for its creeping stems and bright-yellow flowers. The form 'Aureum', with yellow leaves, is better in hanging baskets; it is less vigorous and has prettier foliage.

Impatiens
variegata 'Flora-Plena'

Geranium
'Gala Cherry'

Ivy-leaved
Geranium
'Mexicano'

Small-leaved ivies

LEFT Cascading and trailing foliage plants introduce a framework of permanency to hanging baskets. Also they produce colour early in summer, as well as continuing the display into early autumn. Some plants, such as the asparagus fern *Asparagus densiflorus* 'Sprengeri' are slightly tender while others, like ivy, have a hardy nature.

HOUSEPLANTS IN HANGING BASKETS

In temperate countries, some foliage plants which are normally grown as houseplants can be planted in hanging baskets during summer. However, they are soon damaged by frost and are best reserved for warm positions. Asparagus fern (*Asparagus densiflorus* 'Sprengeri') has wiry, arching stems which bear light to mid-green needle-like leaves. The stems' curving lines visually link other elements of the display. Other plants include the silvery inch plant (*Zebrina pendula*) and the related tradescantias.

More unusual is *Lotus berthelotii*, with a wide range of common names including parrot's beak, coral gem and winged pea. It is a tender perennial, displaying long, trailing stems with silvery, narrow leaves borne in small clusters. Scarlet, pea-like flowers about 2.5cm (1in) long appear in summer. It is native to the Canary Islands.

ABOVE An unpainted brick wall creates a neutrally coloured background for hanging baskets, enabling a wide range of flowers or foliage plants to be displayed. This display is formed mainly of red and pink flowers, toned down by white flowers and green leaves.

CREATING WHITE AND SILVER THEMES

White flowers have a simplicity which appeals to many gardeners, especially in old and long-established gardens, with well-weathered brickwork and stone. Whites relate closely to soft, pale colours. White, palest mauve and faintly blue-tinged flowers harmonize with plants with silver and grey foliage to make fresh, cool-toned displays. Creamy-white flowers merge well with the yellowish tones in golden foliage and leaves with cream and yellow variegation. These displays have a calming influence.

White themes can have a delicate, demure quality, especially when seen in partial shade or when the flowers are not pure white. But in full sun, white displays can be dazzling – especially when they include smooth, gleaming white blooms that reflect maximum amounts of light. Dark backgrounds heighten this effect.

White brightens adjacent colours, which is why multicoloured groupings have so much more impact against white backgrounds. But when creating an all-white feature, avoid a position where neighbours could upstage the carefully orchestrated effect of a display mainly or wholly formed of whites and silvers.

PLANTS WITH WHITE FLOWERS

Many white-flowered plants are white varieties or forms of species with a wide range of other colours.

* The wax begonia (*Begonia semperflorens*) has varieties in a wide range of colours, including reds and pinks. Look for 'Viva', with pure white flowers amid rich bottle-green leaves.

* The Swan River daisy (*Brachyscome iberidifolia*) is a half-hardy annual with large, daisy-like flowers, often in blue tones. 'White Splendour' bears a wealth of white flowers throughout summer; each plant is said to produce more than a hundred blooms.
* The tussock campanula (*Campanula carpatica*) is a perennial easily raised from seed and with the performance

THE EVENING FACTOR

When using plants with large, pure white flowers, remember that in strong sunlight they appear to be even brighter and in very hot countries may be too brilliant. Conversely, in the evening when the strength of the sun diminishes, white flowers and leaves remain visible long after dark blues and reds have faded into the blackness of night. Because of their late-evening visibility, containers full of white plants are ideal for displaying by entrances or flights of steps.

ABOVE The white and pale yellow flowers mixed with all-green and variegated foliage in this hanging basket are pretty and demure and give coverage to a dull brick wall.

of an annual. The variety 'Bellissimo' has a trailing nature ideal for hanging baskets and comes in either blue or white.

Widely known as dwarf morning glory, the hardy annual *Convolvulus tricolor* produces large, bell-like flowers of rich blue. The variety 'White Ensign' has white flowers, each with a yellow throat. It is ideal for trailing over a basket's edge.

THE IMPACT OF WHITENESS

The surface texture of flowers and leaves influences the nature of reflected light and its effect on the eye. Light from a flower with a smooth or waxy surface is purer than that from one that has a papery texture, or a complex shape with shadows between its petals. Flowers in small, clustered heads also reflect less light – and so look less brilliantly white – than ones with larger surfaces. These factors influence the impact of a display.

Single-colour themes always attract attention, whatever the colour of the flowers. Yellow themes are vibrant and burst with life, red arrangements have amorous overtones while white ones are demure. This arrangement of trailing begonias *(Begonia Tuberhybrida)* could be displayed in a porch or lobby as well as outdoors.

Busy Lizzie (*Impatiens walleriana*, earlier known as *I. sultani*) is a popular half-hardy annual for hanging baskets and other containers. There are many named varieties; the hybrid 'Tempo Series' has a white form with flowers up to 5cm (2in) wide on branching, pendulous stems.

Lobelia (*Lobelia erinus*) is grown as a half-hardy annual. Its small flowers on upright or cascading plants are indispensable in hanging baskets. Look for white forms.

Sweet alyssum (*Lobularia maritima*), grown as a half-hardy annual to produce plants early in the year, is still widely known by its earlier name *Alyssum maritimum*. It is available in several colours, including white.

Nemophila maculata '5-spot' is a trailing annual with the lightest of pale-blue flowers, with a deep-blue spot at each petal tip.

Nemophila atomaria 'Snowstorm' is an annual. Its trailing stems are packed with white flowers peppered in small black spots.

Nierembergia 'Mont Blanc' creates masses of cup-shaped white flowers 2.5cm (1in) wide with small, yellow eyes. It trails and flowers throughout summer; dead-heading encourages the development of more flowers.

Petunias (*Petunia × hybrida*) always create a splendid succession of flowers in summer. 'Super Cascade Improved Mixed' has a cascading habit that is ideal for hanging baskets and comes in many colours. Select the white-flowered form to drench hanging baskets in beautiful white trumpets from early summer to autumn.

CREATING YELLOW THEMES

Yellow is highly visible, the brightest colour of all. A hanging basket filled with yellow *Calceolaria integrifolia* 'Sunshine', one of the slipper or pouch flowers, immediately captures attention and makes a focal point. But yellow can be more complex. Yellows include paler creams, demure primrose and fresh lemon-yellow on one side, deepening through old-gold to orange and bronze tones on the other. A medley of these yellows set among green leaves makes a lively picture. To soften the sharp contrast between the lightness of yellow and the darker greens, add touches of brighter green foliage – a colour midway between the two: the fresh green of golden creeping Jenny, or the muted lime-green of *Helichrysum petiolare* 'Aureum' both fit the bill.

Warm yellow plus neighbouring orange and hot scarlet-red together create a fiery radiance. This combination can work surprisingly well against the related tones of a red-brick background, but would glow more hotly against the contrast of a white or grey wall.

PLANTS TO CONSIDER

Yellow is the colour of spring, when window boxes, tubs and troughs are rich in gleaming daffodils, crocus and polyanthus. The range of sunshine-yellow flowers for summer hanging baskets is perhaps smaller, but there are some interesting yellows to choose from. For yellow themes, set them against foliage plants such as the yellow-leaved creeping Jenny (*Lysimachia nummularia* 'Aurea'), which itself has bright-yellow flowers, or the lime-green *Helichrysum petiolare* 'Aureum' (or 'Limelight'), described on pages 26 and 27. Small-leaved ivies with yellow and green variegated leaves are also a possibility.

Antirrhinums, widely known as snapdragons, are usually

This hanging basket has been filled with Pansy 'Universal Yellow'. The deep yellow of the velvety flowers looks stunning against the green leaves and the moss creates an interesting textural background.

RIGHT **Yellow-themed hanging baskets create beacons of colour at entrances. Some displays are formed of a dense array of flowers, such as with *Calceolaria integrifolia* 'Sunshine' (see *opposite page*), while others have yellow flowers that create a wispy and more airy display (right) that does not immediately capture attention but is more likely to retain interest throughout summer.**

BASKETS AGAINST GREY STONE WALLS

Grey stone walls are not dominant and create soft, relaxing backgrounds for plants with pink, red, deep-purple and deep-blue flowers. A combination of petunias, geraniums (pelargoniums) and the blue-flowered star of Bethlehem *Campanula isophylla* create a spectacular display.

raised as half-hardy annuals and create feasts of colour in window boxes and troughs. Short varieties can be used in hanging baskets. 'Sweetheart' is a low-growing variety, while slightly taller and suitable only for large baskets is 'Yellow Monarch'. Their flowers last from the latter part of early summer to the onset of frosts in autumn.

• The basket begonia (*Begonia × tuberhybrida* 'Pendula') is well-known for its pendulous habit and double flowers. The wide range of varieties includes several yellow ones. Rose-like flowers 5–7.5cm (2–3in) wide appear from early summer to early autumn.

• The slipper flower is best known in temperate regions as a houseplant, but there are more resilient species which can be grown outdoors in hanging baskets in sheltered positions. *Calceolaria integrifolia* 'Sunshine' creates a mass of small, golden-yellow, pouch-like flowers.

• Pansies (*Viola × wittrockiana*) have some of the brightest and most dramatic of all flowers. The large blooms that look like faces always gain attention. Choose varieties such as the free-flowering 'Rhine Gold' with yellow flowers distinctively blotched black, or 'Flame Princess' with rich, clear-yellow to cream flowers blotched scarlet to mahogany. There are also varieties with very attractive plain yellow blooms, both large and small.

• *Tagetes tenuifolia pumila*, a form of marigold, has slender stems, sweet-smelling leaves and masses of 2.5cm (1in) wide yellow flowers.

Yellow *Begonia* × *tuberhybrida*

Geranium 'Gala Cherry'

Ivy-leaved *Geranium* 'Lachskoinigen'

New Guinea *Impatiens*

Felicia amelloides

ABOVE Deep-yellow begonias mixed with pink and red geraniums make a colourful, though not overpowering display of flowers and foliage.

RIGHT Sometimes, yellow-theme hanging baskets are not totally formed of yellow flowers or leaves. Instead, a few dominantly sized shaped and coloured flowers create the yellow theme. Such boldly flowered plants include *Begonia × tuberhybrida* and its pendulous offspring the basket begonia (*B. × t.* 'Pendula').

CREATING BLUE THEMES

The spectrum of blues offers many possibilities, from misty, delicate tints to deep, vibrant tones. Pure, clear blue is a summer colour, associated with radiant skies where no clouds threaten. Emotionally it is thus a colour of coolness and tranquillity. In its more intense versions this pure blue deepens to the vivid blue of gentians. Both look beautiful and show up best against pale yellows, creams, whites and greys. They contrast brilliantly with bright yellow, orange and red.

Many of the blues, however, are not clear and cool but warm-toned, moving along the colour spectrum towards indigo, violet and red. Paler tints of these warm blues veer towards lavender and mauve. The darker versions blend into violet. The hint of red pigment in these blues makes them combine well with crimson. The paler pastel lilac-blues make gentle, soft effects with mauves, pinks and greys. Deeper, darker warm blues combine with stronger reds and crimsons in a dominant, glowing intensity.

In baskets blue works well in both its gentle, diffused mood and its strong, dominant role. Some trailing lobelias are a lightly washed blue, while the 'Blue Ensign' morning glory has large, dark trumpets, each with a white centre. Both have backgrounds which suit them: soft, light blue against red bricks; dark blue in front of grey.

**PLANTS WITH
BLUE FLOWERS**
There are blue flowers of many descriptions from which to choose flowers for hanging baskets in summer.
Anagallis linifolia 'Gentian Blue' creates a dramatic picture, with masses of 12–18mm (½–¾in) wide glowing deep-blue flowers with golden stamens. The display lasts throughout summer and is ideal for creating colour at the edges of baskets.
Brachyscome iberidifolia 'Blue Star' produces a mass of light-blue, daisy-like flowers ideal for the top of a large basket. A more violet-toned variety of swan river daisy, 'Purple Splendour', is particularly floriferous: as with 'White Splendour', each plant is said to produce more than one hundred flowers, creating a spectacular display.

Campanula carpatica 'Bellissimo', like the Swan River daisy, has both white- and blue-flowered forms. The latter develops chalice-shaped papery flowers of a gentle blue. By nature it is a trailing hardy perennial, but it is usually

BELOW *Campanula poscharskyana* is a vigorous, spreading perennial usually raised from seeds. From early summer to late autumn it bears lavender-blue, star-like flowers about 2.5cm (1in) wide. When planted in a hanging basket it creates a dominant display, and the plant is just as attractive in a wall basket.

grown as a half-hardy annual for plants early in the year. In autumn, plants can be removed and planted into a garden.

* *Convolvulus tricolor* 'Blue Ensign' is a vivid blue-flowered form of morning glory. The 5cm (2in) wide trumpet-like flowers have white centres. A mass of these flowers turns a hanging basket into a focal point. A few blooms add vitality without becoming too overpowering.

* Lobelias are the mainstays of the blue candidates for containers. Whether bushy or cascading, light or dark, plain or white-eyed, they grace any hanging basket. There are many named forms to choose from. *Lobelia erinus* 'Blue Cascade' is a pastel blue that is more companionable than strong, dominating blues when mixed with other plants. Its demure quality also attracts attention when the plant is used on its own.

* Petunias have large, trumpet-shaped flowers from early summer to the frosts of autumn. The range of *Petunia × hybrida* is wide and includes pendulous types that flood containers with colour. 'Super Cascade Improved Mixed' is available in mixed and individual colours, including a range of blues. Most have slightly warmish tones, tending towards lavender when pale and towards violet when dark, and they blend beautifully with mauves, pinks, reds and whites.

* *Campanula isophylla* (star of Bethlehem) is frequently grown in porches and lobbies, as well as outdoors during summer. Star-shaped, 2.5cm (1in) wide blue flowers appear during late summer and early autumn amid heart-shaped mid-green leaves.

BELOW Blue-coloured themes are not so dramatic as yellow, but they are very welcome as a change from vibrant reds, eye-catching yellows or demure white-and-green arrangement. There are many blue-coloured plants to choose from and many are featured on this and the previous page.

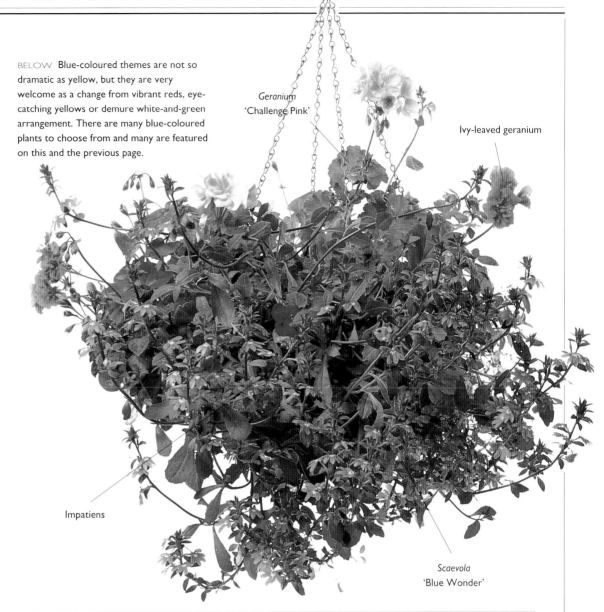

Geranium 'Challenge Pink'

Ivy-leaved geranium

Impatiens

Scaevola 'Blue Wonder'

BASKETS AGAINST DARK BACKGROUNDS

Dark walls and fences and other gloomy areas especially benefit from displays of brightly coloured flowers and foliage. Bold, dramatic clusters with contrasting colours have the greatest impact. The white, mauve and purple petunias mixed with *Helichrysum petiolatum* here create an eye-catching hanging basket against a black-painted fence. Bright flower combinations like this will brighten any dark background.

CREATING PINK AND RED THEMES

The reds can be romantic: full-blooded red has a hot and passionate nature, while blush-pink is warm and demure. They are closely related: a pink is a desaturated red. The paler the pink, the more white it contains and the smaller the amount of red pigment in its make up. The stronger reds are more assertive. Red flowers against a mid-green background assume a three-dimensional nature, appearing to stand out from the green foliage. This colour dominates its neighbours, especially when used in large masses.

A useful guide when choosing reds for a scheme is to assess whether they are warm- or cool-toned. Warm, scarlet-red harmonizes with orange and yellow and creates 'hot' mixtures. Paler versions include peach- and salmon-pinks, which also blend into softer yellows and oranges. The 'cool' reds have a bluish cast and include crimson and magenta, while the cool pinks sometimes border on lilac and lavender tones. Both blend well in schemes with cold whites, blues and violets.

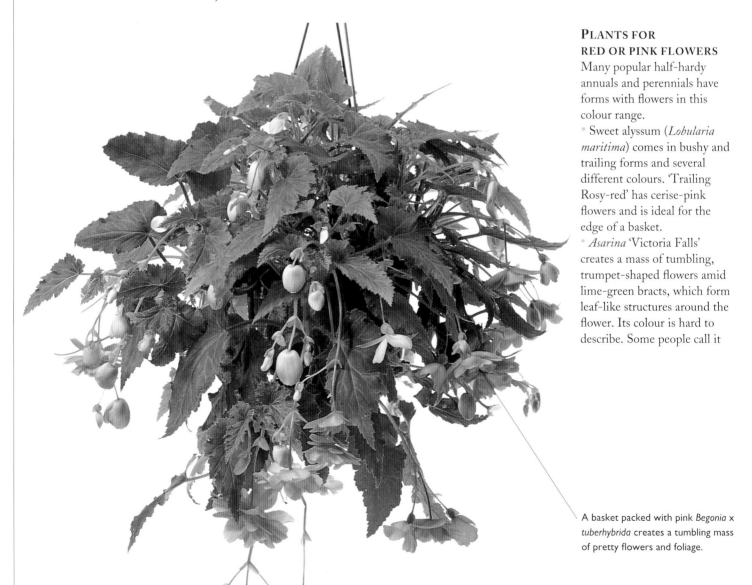

A basket packed with pink *Begonia* x *tuberhybrida* creates a tumbling mass of pretty flowers and foliage.

PLANTS FOR RED OR PINK FLOWERS

Many popular half-hardy annuals and perennials have forms with flowers in this colour range.

• Sweet alyssum (*Lobularia maritima*) comes in bushy and trailing forms and several different colours. 'Trailing Rosy-red' has cerise-pink flowers and is ideal for the edge of a basket.

• *Asarina* 'Victoria Falls' creates a mass of tumbling, trumpet-shaped flowers amid lime-green bracts, which form leaf-like structures around the flower. Its colour is hard to describe. Some people call it

FUCHSIAS FOR HANGING BASKETS

Fuchsias always capture attention and to many eyes are the aristocrats of container planting. Some have single flowers, with just four petals, while semi-double types have five, six or seven. Double types have eight or more petals. Fuchsias especially suited to hanging baskets include:

✳ 'Cascade': Single flowers with white sepals flushed carmine, and deep-red petals.

✳ 'Falling Stars': Single flowers, with pale-scarlet sepals and turkey-red petals with slight orange tints.

✳ 'Lena': Semi-double flowers, with rose-magenta petals flushed pink.

✳ 'Marinka': Single flowers, with rich-red sepals and dark-red petals.

✳ 'Swingtime': Double flowers, with shiny-red sepals and milky-white petals.

are two-coloured. Be sure to plant cascading fuchsias rather than varieties with a bushy habit. For a selection of those recommended for planting in hanging baskets, see left.

○ *Impatiens walleriana*, the well-known busy Lizzie, is a parent of many hybrids and creates a wealth of flowers in many colours, including shades of blush, rose and scarlet. There are many varieties, such as the Tempo Series.

○ *Lobelia erinus* 'Cascade Mixed' is a series of trailing forms, ideal for softening the edges of baskets. They include a range of colours such as lilac and crimson.

○ Nasturtiums (*Tropaeolum majus*), climbing and trailing plants well-known for orange and yellow flowers, make vibrant displays in hanging baskets. Some varieties have deep-red and scarlet flowers.

○ Ivy-leaved geraniums (*Pelargonium peltatum*) and the Cascade varieties are hanging basket classics for their red or pink flowers amid shapely trailing foliage.

○ Petunias are invaluable, in mixed and single colours. The 'Super Cascade Improved Mixed' variety has several forms in the pink to red range, including pale, delicate pinks, vibrant cerise, rich crimson and warm red. The cascading plants soon fill baskets with colour. Petunias flower prolifically and soon drench hanging baskets with large, trumpet-like flowers.

cerise-purple; others see it as a dark, warm pink. It is a matter of perception, often affected by the strength of light in which it is seen.

○ *Begonia × tuberhybrida* 'Show Angels' are hybrids in a range of separate colours including rose-pink. The pendulous flowers are mostly double and drench hanging baskets with colour throughout summer. 'Clips Mixed', another hybrid, has double flowers often 6cm (2½ in) wide. It is available in both mixed and separate colours, including pink and scarlet. Each plant produces up to forty flowers, with flowering curtailed only by the onset of frost in autumn.

○ Cascading fuchsias are popular as centre-pieces in hanging baskets, with small and bushy plants set immediately around them and trailing types on the outside. You can choose from a wealth of colour variations that is all the wider because most flowers

LEFT A display primarily of red flowers creates a dominant feature, especially when in strong sunlight. Cascading red begonias and petunias are dramatic plants and need to be tempered by the inclusion of a few foliage plants and white flowers.

BELOW Pink can be introduced into many colour arrangements. It is a non-aggressive shade and can be used in medleys of colour as well as single themes.

HANGING BASKETS IN LOBBIES AND PORCHES

During summer, lobbies and porches provide homes for many of the hardier houseplants. Some, such as ivies, can be left there throughout the year. The decision whether to cosset a houseplant indoors or to put it in a porch or lobby – or even to move it outside in summer – is a matter of geography and aspect. Sometimes a difference in latitude of a mere hundred miles turns a houseplant into one for outdoors, or vice versa. And within the same area a warm, sheltered site is kinder to borderline plants than one exposed to chill winds. Check your local conditions. For example, the pig-a-back plant (*Tolmiea menziesii*) is hardy enough to be left outside all year in most temperate regions, but it may retain its foliage better under shelter. Conversely, creeping Jenny (*Lysimachia nummularia*) is often grown in lobbies and porches, but can thrive very well outdoors.

ABOVE The spider plant (*Chlorophytum elatum* 'Vittatum') also known as St. Bernard's lily, soon adapts to a hanging basket.

INDOOR HANGING BASKETS

The majority of outdoor hanging baskets are formed of a plastic-covered wire frame. For lobbies and porches (and indoors), solid plastic baskets are the best choice as most are fitted with a drip-tray to prevent water falling on the floor. In these types there is also the choice of either re-planting the plants in compost in the basket, or leaving them in their pots, placing them inside the basket and packing moist peat around the pot. The latter has the advantage that new plants can be easily added. It also allows tender plants to be moved from draughty to warm rooms in late autumn. When planting directly into the basket, choose varieties that share about the same degree of hardiness.

ABOVE Hanging baskets formed totally of busy Lizzies create spectacular displays in slightly shady porches and lobbies, as well as in well-ventilated conservatories, where the temperature can be prevented from soaring upwards. When grown in a lobby, porch or conservatory the compost soon dries and if this happens plants suffer; if neglect continues, plants will die.

FOLIAGE PLANTS FOR PORCHES AND LOBBIES

* *Callisia elegans* (striped inch plant)
* *Cissus rhombifolia* 'Ellen Danica' (mermaid vine)
* *Cyanotis kewensis* (teddy bear plant)
* *Ficus pumila* 'Sonny' (variegated creeping fig)
* *Ficus radicans* 'Variegata' (trailing fig)
* *Lysimachia nummularia* 'Aurea' (golden creeping Jenny or moneywort)
* *Mikania ternata* (plush vine)
* *Nephrolepis exaltata* (ladder fern)
* *Oplismenus hirtellus* 'Variegatus'
* *Pellaea rotundifolia* (New Zealand brake fern)
* *Peperomia scandens* 'Variegata'
* *Saxifraga sarmentosa* 'Tricolor' (strawberry geranium)
* *Sedum morganianum* (donkey's tail or burro's tail)
* *Selaginella uncinata* (peacock moss)
* *Soleirolia soleirolii* (mind your own business)
* *Stenotaphrum secundatum* 'Variegatum'
* *Tolmiea menziesii* (pig-a-back plant)
* *Tradescantia fluminensis* 'Variegata' (wandering Jew)
* *Zebrina pendula* (silvery inch plant)

LEFT Hanging baskets formed of
plastic and with drip-trays built into
their base are ideal for use in lobbies
and porches. Plants can be planted in
the basket, or left in their pots and
just stood in the hanging basket,
with moist peat packed around
them. This allows rapid changes of
plants, should any deteriorate.

Chlorophytum comosum 'Variegatum'

Nephrolepis 'Bostonensis'

Small-leaved ivies

Peperomia hederifolia

USING ANNUALS

Many of the flowering annuals
featured on pages 54 to 61 can be
grown in lobbies and porches,
provided the temperature does not
rise too dramatically and the
compost is kept moist. Open
porches, which are cooler than
closed lobbies, are more suitable.

RIGHT The plume asparagus
(*Asparagus densiflorus* 'Myers',
sometimes known as
A. meyeri) creates feathery,
light-green plumes that can
be highlighted by positioning
small-leaved ivies around the
container's edge.

WALL BASKETS AND MANGERS

Wall baskets and mangers create magnificent displays against walls of all kinds. Planting them is described in detail on page 49. Like other container features, they are especially attractive when colour co-ordinated with their surroundings. It is easier to grow plants in wall baskets and mangers than hanging baskets; this is because they hold more compost and there is less risk of the compost rapidly becoming dry. Also, the plants are slightly protected by a wall. Positioning wall baskets is discussed on the opposite page; few gardens cannot accommodate at least one of them.

Wall baskets are becoming increasingly popular and are available in a wide range of sizes (*see page 65*). Once the basket is secured to a wall it can be left in position for several years. However, it is necessary to inspect it thoroughly at least once a year to ensure its fixings are secure.

ABOVE Impatiens (busy Lizzie) creates a blanket of colour. There are many varieties and plants can be raised from seeds sown in late winter or early spring in gentle warmth.

RIGHT As well as securing wall pots to walls, they can also be used to brighten bland fencing. Indeed, it is easier to secure these containers to wood than to brick, when drilling is necessary and strong wall fixings are essential. This pot is packed with begonias.

ABOVE As well as creating single-colour themes, introduce a central and dominant plant, with a sea of plants around it. Here is a tuberous-rooted begonia with a mass of impatiens around it. These displays can create either harmonies or contrasts.

ABOVE White walls highlight many colours, but ensure that water cannot pass through the compost and then run down the wall. Here is a medley of plants and colours, with marigolds in the top and a range of trailers around it.

POSITIONING
WALL BASKETS

Like window boxes, wall baskets are secured to buildings and therefore leave the floor area underneath bare. In some gardens this is a bonus as plants in tubs, urns and troughs can be grouped around them to create a more interesting display. It is also a blessing to place them along the front of a mews cottage, where a road or pavement butts on a house wall. By leaving the paved area underneath a wall basket free of containers, rubbish which accumulates can be removed and the surfaced hosed.

There are many ways to combine wall baskets with other containers. Perhaps the simplest is to position a large tub on either side of a waist-high basket. Plant them with a bushy or half-standard fuchsia to create height and to act as a

frame for the basket. Position the tubs so that the plants slightly overlap the edges of the wall basket.

At the fronts of houses, where flower-beds are under windows, wall baskets create colour along bare walls. Use two small wall baskets, one either side of a window and, for extra colour, a window box could be added.

Small wall baskets are also ideal at the sides of front doors and for added colour position one above the other, but beware of water dripping on the lower one. Bright-faced, happy-looking pansies are excellent in these positions as they do not encroach on surrounding space.

Plastic and terracotta wall baskets are better than wire-framed types on balconies as they do not readily drip excess water. Position them on either side of a sliding balcony door;

make sure that hinged doors do not hide or squash flowers when opened.

Where front doors are deeply recessed into a house and perhaps with overhanging brickwork, plastic and terracotta wall baskets are ideal as they do not protrude far from a wall.

Where wall baskets on balconies are under cover and

not exposed to rain, ensure they are regularly watered. The amount of compost in plastic and terracotta types is limited and the compost soon dries, especially when in strong and direct sunlight.

Wall baskets also enable disabled people to garden; they can be easily reached from wheelchairs and do not involve the gardener in bending down.

CHOOSING WALL BASKETS AND MANGERS

Mangers come in a range of sizes, from 30cm (12in) wide to 72cm (28in), in increases of about 10cm (4in). Wire-framed wall baskets range in width from 23cm (9in) to 50cm (20in), plastic and terracotta types from 15cm (6in) to 25cm (10in). Plastic and terracotta baskets are ideal for placing one above another, and especially where it is essential that water should not drip on plants or surfaces below.

GROWING FOOD PLANTS IN BASKETS

To gardeners with a large vegetable plot, food plants in hanging baskets and wall baskets are superfluous. But for balcony, courtyard and patio gardeners they may offer the only chance of fresh, home-grown food. Besides, the plants – and their glistening fruits – have visual appeal and help to create distinctive features.

The constraints of growing food in hanging baskets and wall baskets are greater than when using tubs and growing-bags. There is less compost, especially in hanging baskets; water may be needed several times a day in strong sunlight, and regular feeding is needed. For success, be sure to use suitable varieties.

Wall baskets offer more opportunities to grow food than hanging baskets, which are mainly used for strawberries, tomatoes and small culinary herbs. Although hanging baskets have their limitations, they do have one advantage over other containers on a patio – plants in them are inaccessible to slugs and snails. Plants in wall baskets may also need protection from these pests. Gravel chippings in a narrow bed at the base of the wall serve as a deterrent. Alternatively, use slug bait.

HANGING BASKETS

Strawberries, tomatoes and a few small culinary herbs can be cultivated successfully in hanging baskets. They are grown in summer only; in autumn the crop and the compost are removed and the basket stored in a shed. It is possible to encourage the herbs to continue growing until early winter by placing the basket in a greenhouse.

• Strawberries are normally increased from runners which are encouraged to root and later moved to their growing positions. However, the variety 'Temptation' is raised annually from seed.

It is possible to raise your own plants by sowing seed in gentle warmth in late winter or early spring, but much easier and more convenient to buy a few established plants in late spring or early summer. Plant them in a hanging basket and put it outside when all risk of major frost has passed. A few sheets of newspaper will prevent a slight frost damaging them even after planting.

This variety has a slightly trailing habit and produces sweet and juicy fruits from mid-summer to the frosts of autumn. Pick ripe fruits regularly to encourage the development of further ones.

• The tomato variety 'Tumbler' is specially suited for growing in hanging baskets, where it cascades and produces sweet, cherry-like fruits 2.5cm (1in) across from mid-summer to the frosts of autumn.

Either buy established plants in late spring or early summer, or sow seeds 1.5mm ($\frac{1}{16}$in) deep in spring, about five to seven weeks before you plan to plant them and place outdoors in frost-free situation. Germination takes up to two weeks in 21–24°C (70–75°F). When large enough to handle, transfer the seedlings to individual, 6–7.5cm (2½–3in) wide pots. Lower the

LEFT This pretty herb-filled windowbox would be perfect for a kitchen window. And with the window open a gentle breeze would fill the room with a delicate fragrance.

GROWING HERBS

Herbs will grow in both hanging baskets and wall baskets. Small, bushy types can be planted directly into the compost, but most herbs are better just left in their pots and positioned in the container, with moist peat packed around them. This allows plants to be changed whenever they become too large or invasive, or if they run to seed. Pots of chives, parsley, common and variegated sages, basil, pot marigolds, balm, thyme and savory can be used.

temperature and acclimatize plants to outdoor conditions. Incidentally, loam-based composts produce shorter plants than peat-based types and for that reason are better when raising this variety for planting in hanging baskets. Put one plant in a 30cm (1ft) wide basket, and two or three in a 45cm (1½ft) or larger container. The plants are naturally bushy and do not need to have sideshoots removed in the same way as cordon types grown in greenhouses and gardens.

* Herbs (*see page 66*).

WALL BASKETS

Because they are usually larger, these hold more compost than hanging baskets and so offer the opportunity to grow a wider range of food plants, including the following:

* Tomatoes can be raised and grown in the same way as in hanging baskets; use the same variety or another bush type. Do not use cordon types, which grow upwards and need to be supported.

When planting them, set plants about 30cm (1ft) apart. Ensure the top of the soil-ball is level with the compost's surface. Firm compost around it and thoroughly but gently water the compost to ensure it settles around the roots.

* Cucumbers such as 'Bush Champion' can be planted in wall baskets. The compact plants produce cucumbers up to 25cm (10in) long, which dangle conveniently from the basket. From being planted, cucumbers can be cut in as little as eight weeks and these continue bearing fruits until late summer.

Plants can be raised by sowing seeds singly and about 12mm (½in) deep in small pots of peat-based compost in early or mid-spring at 20–24°C (68–75°F). After germination, lower the temperature slightly, keeping the compost moist but not continually saturated. Slowly acclimatize plants to outdoor temperatures and plant into wall baskets as soon as the risk of frost has passed. Put one plant in a small wall basket; alternatively use two or three in a large manger.

* The sweet pepper 'Redskin' is ideal for wall baskets. It has a bushy habit, grows up to 40cm (16in) high and produces large, rich-red fruits. It needs a warm, sheltered position. Either buy established plants and put them into wall baskets as soon as the risk of frost has passed, or sow seeds in the

same way as described for cucumbers. Position plants 30–38cm (12–15in) apart.

* Courgettes form compact, bushy plants that yield small fruits over a long period. They usually start to crop within sixty days of being planted. They can be raised in the same way as cucumbers.

* The Cos-type lettuce 'Little Gem' is compact and ideal for containers. By making successional sowings from spring to mid-summer, lettuces can be harvested from mid-summer to autumn. Ensure the compost in the wall basket is fertile, lightly disturb it with a hand-fork, level and water the surface. The following day, thinly sow seeds 12mm (½in) deep in drills 15cm (6in) apart. When seedlings are large enough to handle, thin them 15cm (6in) apart.

HERBS IN PLANTERS

Herbs can be planted in hanging baskets and wall baskets, but often it is more convenient to put them in a planter with cup-shaped positions around its side. This enables many different herbs to be grown in the same container and acts as a moisture collector when placed outside to take advantage of the climate.

The selection here includes chives, savory, thyme, sage, basil and balm.

The herbs can be removed and replanted when they become too large and they are always ready to hand when the cook needs them.

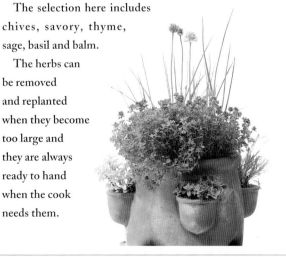

A pot of herbs positioned outside a kitchen door not only makes a colourful display but is also useful for culinary purposes.

TUBS, POTS, URNS AND PLANTERS

Tubs and urns create major features, while clusters of plants in pots produce a varied display. These containers vary widely in shape and size and the types of plants that suit them. Large tubs are ideal for shrubs such as rhododendrons, hydrangeas and conifers, as well as summer-flowering bedding plants and spring-flowering bulbs. Urns are smaller but usually gain attention through their shape and position, perhaps on a plinth or by a flight of steps. They are perhaps best devoted to summer-flowering plants and displays of bulbs in spring.

Pots, when grouped, have a Mediterranean feel and can be filled with ephemeral summer flowers, herbs or plants that are sufficiently resilient to be displayed on a patio during summer but need the comfort of a frost-proof greenhouse in winter. These range from the succulent and variegated *Agave americana* 'Variegata' to pelargoniums and palms (*see left*).

THE GRAND SCENE

Stone urns are reminiscent of earlier times, when gardening was often on the grand scale. Elevated lawns, wide flights of steps and long vistas were often punctuated with shapely urns in a variety of forms, shapes and sizes. Some had broad tops and were designed to be seen mainly from above, their centres packed with bright, upward-looking flowers, while those on pedestals had ornate outlines and a shape best viewed from the side. Cascading plants were featured in them. There were even cask-like urns intended solely as architectural features, with no opportunity to use plants in them. These are especially attractive when combined with low lavender hedges, perhaps set on a bank skirting a lawn.

Plastic and glassfibre urns, often used today in place of traditional stone types, are less

ABOVE **A feast of colour in pots in a small garden.**
OPPOSITE **Placing tender plants in decorative containers outside introduces a further dimension. Large and attractive foliage plants such as palms are soon damaged by frost but create superb summer displays in warm and sheltered areas.**

costly, lighter and have considerable potential, especially when displayed at some distance, with both bushy and cascading plants cleverly planted to mask their synthetic origins.

The distinctive and dramatic shape of urns makes them look best alone. Rather than clustering them like pots, position them singly or in pairs to highlight any special garden features, mark a focal point or to lead the eye towards a distant point of interest.

Clay pots and planters, on the other hand, have an informal and more functional nature and a medley of them in various sizes, each filled with a different plant, creates a relaxed feature.

Wooden tubs, too, are less formal and suitable for a patio or small back yard. Filled with brightly coloured flowers or fruit their natural, rustic appearance is charming.

PLANTING TUBS

Tubs form dominant and impressive features; their size alone gives them a distinction and presence achieved by few other containers. Their large size calls for bold and dramatic displays, whether formed by a handsome shrub such as the variegated *Aucuba japonica* 'Variegata', or a mass of spring bulbs or summer-flowering bedding plants.

Miniature bulbs – and especially those that flower in winter and spring – are best reserved for small containers such as stone sinks and small urns. It is large trumpet-faced daffodils, short-stemmed tulips and stocky, soldier-like hyacinths that are the prime bulb candidates for planting and growing in tubs.

Summer-flowering displays need bold colours and a central plant that will create height and assist in balancing the size of the tub. *Abutilon pictum* 'Thompsonii', with green, maple-like leaves heavily spotted yellow and intriguing orange flowers, is ideal as a central feature. A large or half-standard fuchsia could also be used.

PLANTING BULBS

Plant spring-flowering bulbs, such as daffodils, tulips and hyacinths, in early autumn, as soon as they are available. Always buy the best quality bulbs as it is essential to produce a concentrated display. In gardens, bulbs that do not flower are usually not too noticeable, as others close by continue the display. But in a tub, bulbs that fail to flower are conspicuous and mar the impact of the whole.

Space out the bulbs before planting them; position the tallest varieties in the centre.

LEFT Before planting a tub with bulbs, thoroughly clean it and check that the drainage holes are free. Position it on three strong bricks or pieces of broken paving stone to ensure surplus water can drain freely from holes in the base. This also deters slugs and snails. Then, plant the bulbs see above. Do not try to move the tub after it has been planted – it will be too heavy.

Ensure the tub's base has a few drainage holes, then fill with 5cm (2in) of clean rubble or pebbles. Add and gently firm loam-based compost to within 2.5cm (1in) of the rim.

Spread out the bulbs on the surface of the compost: space daffodils and tulips with 5cm (2in) between them; 7.5cm (3in) for hyacinths. Use a trowel to plant daffodils, tulips and hyacinths, so that their noses are covered by 10–13cm (4–5in) of compost. Firm compost over them and thoroughly water it. The surface of the compost will settle slightly to about 5cm (2in) below the rim.

Position the top level of bulbs between the necks of the lower ones. Firm compost over them.

After the bulbs are planted, the noses of the top bulbs are covered with about 10cm (4in) of compost.

After planting, leave the top of the compost about 2.5cm (1in) below the rim. Later, this will settle.

Space out the lower level of bulbs on firm compost, 20cm (8in) below the tub's rim.

Well-drained compost

A 5cm (2in) layer of pebbles or clean rubble over drainage holes in the tub's base

DOUBLE LAYERS

Large tubs densely packed with bright-yellow daffodils create a memorable display, especially when positioned against a white or a dark wall.

To produce a tub packed with flowers, plant the bulbs in two layers. Check the drainage holes in the tub's base, then fill with 5cm (2in) of pebbles or clean rubble. Add and firm a layer of compost, so that its top is about 20cm (8in) below the tub's rim. Space daffodil bulbs 7.5cm (3in) apart. Add and firm further compost between the bulbs until only their noses can be seen. Then, place a further row of bulbs between them. Add more compost until it is about 2.5cm (1in) below the tub's top. Then thoroughly water the compost.

PLANTING BEDDING PLANTS

1 When planting summer-flowering bedding plants, first position the tub on three bricks; check the drainage holes are open and fill the base with pebbles. Add a thick layer of peat to help retain moisture and top up to within 2.5cm (1in) of the rim with compost. Then, position plants – still in their pots – on top. Put a large plant in the centre and small, bushy types around it.

Plant from the centre outwards.

2 When the positions of the plants are right, put in the main, central one first. Carefully remove the pot and use a trowel to make a hole large enough to accommodate its roots. Position the plant only slightly deeper than before, then gently firm compost around the roots. Add the rest of the plants, but not nearer than 5cm (2in) to the sides. Should watering be neglected, this is where the soil first becomes dry.

IMPROVING SOIL FOR COMPOST

Buying proprietary compost to fill a large tub can be prohibitively expensive. An alternative way is to improve some topsoil from your garden. Select an area free from perennial weeds, such as couch grass, bindweed and horsetail, and that has not recently been converted from pasture land. Spread the soil on a clean surface and mix it with equal parts of sharp sand and moist peat. Ensure they are well-mixed and then use this for planting bulbs, shrubs and small trees. For summer-flowering bedding plants it is safer to use compost that is known to be free from soil pests, which would soon devastate soft and tender plants – do not risk healthy plants in poor compost.

PLANTING A SHRUB

1 When planting a shrub or small tree in a tub it is vital to choose well-drained yet moisture-retentive compost as the roots will soon die unless the excess moisture can escape. Equally, if it dries out the roots will be damaged.

Place the tub on three bricks with the drainage holes clear. Form a 5cm (2in) thick layer of pebbles and the same of moist peat. Add compost and firm it to form a slight mound. When planting a container-grown plant, remove the container and place the soil-ball on the mound with its top slightly lower than before. When planting is complete, the soil surface should be about 2.5cm (1in) below the tub's rim.

2 Check that the most attractive side of the plant is facing outwards – gently revolve the plant until it looks right. Carefully spread compost around the root-ball, ensuring the shrub or tree remains upright. Firm soil in layers around the roots. Make sure that the compost is evenly firmed, otherwise some parts will dry out earlier than others.

When planting is complete, the surface of the compost should be 2.5cm (1in) below the rim. Thoroughly water the compost to settle it around the root-ball. Later, the compost will settle slightly, but this is natural and not a problem as more soil can be added during the following months.

PLANTING TIMES

Tubs provide long-term homes for shrubs and small trees, whereas for spring-flowering bulbs and summer-flowering bedding plants they are used for only six or so months.

• A container-grown shrub or small tree can be planted out into a garden throughout the year, whenever the weather allows. But for planting into a tub, it is best to choose spring or early summer. This is because in winter the soil in tubs may become too wet or frozen; established trees and small shrubs can withstand this if protected (*see pages 72 and 73*), but young ones planted in winter are more susceptible to damage from frost and excessive moisture.

• Spring-flowering bulbs are planted in autumn, as soon as they are available from garden centres and bulb specialists.

• Summer-flowering bedding plants are soon damaged by frost and therefore cannot be planted until late spring or early summer, as soon as the weather is free from frost. Unlike hanging baskets, which can be moved into a greenhouse or conservatory at night if frost is forecast, tubs are too heavy to move once they are planted.

PROTECTING SHRUBS AND TREES IN TUBS

Low temperatures, cold winds and excessive rain threaten shrubs and small trees in tubs during winter. And because gardeners tend to plant slightly delicate plants in tubs, they are especially in danger when temperatures plummet and rain persists for several months.

Removing plants in relatively small pots to a more congenial area is possible, but most large tubs cannot be moved. The alternative is to cover the compost to prevent it becoming excessively wet and to clad the foliage of tender evergreen shrubs in straw.

Centuries ago, large estates grew tender fruiting plants like oranges in large, heavy tubs which were kept under cover in autumn and taken outdoors in spring or early summer. These plants were called 'greens' (i.e., evergreens), hence the name 'greenhouse' for the place where they were sheltered. They were moved on low, four-wheeled trolleys with the aid of plenty of assistance.

KNOCKING OFF SNOW

If snow is left on shrubs and trees it eventually weighs down branches and seriously disfigures them. Use a thick stick or plastic piping to gently tap off the snow.

_1_ During winter, the compost in tubs can become excessively wet and cause roots of shrubs and trees to decay. Wet compost is also likely to freeze and cause further damage. Covering the compost with polythene protects the plants.

_2_ To ensure that the plastic forms a slight slope from the centre of the tub to the outside, place two heavy items on either side of the stem.

_3_ Cut a slit in the polythene, from the outside to the centre, and place it over the compost. Ensure the centre fits snugly around the stem, then cross one flap over the other so that the compost is completely covered.

_4_ Carefully draw the polythene up and around the plant's stem, so that a piece of string can be wrapped around it and tied gently. Take care not to throttle it.

_5_ Overlap the cut ends of the polythene and use stout string to tie it around the tub, 7.5–10cm (3–4in) below the rim. Several separate wrappings of string will ensure it is secure.

The prime purpose of covering the compost is to prevent it from becoming wet, but it is also essential that the compost does dry out during mild winters. Therefore, do not cover the compost with polythene too early in winter and ensure it is removed before growth begins in early spring. During dry winters, check that the compost is evenly moist.

_6_ When the polythene is securely tied, use scissors to cut off the polythene about 10cm (4in) below the string.

In earlier times – before the introduction of polythene – large slates were used to prevent compost becoming too wet. Two slates were needed for each tub, each of them a half-moon hole cut out. The slates were placed at an angle against the plant, the circular hole around the stem and the other side resting on the tub. When both slates were in position a piece of string could be looped over them and tied to bricks.

PROTECTING EVERGREENS

ABOVE The gold-dust plant or spotted laurel, *Aucuba japonica* 'Variegata' (sometimes named 'Maculata'), is a superb shrub for growing in a tub. The shiny green leaves are irregularly spotted with bright gold. During winter it is highlighted by snow but, unfortunately, if left in place this causes damage.

1 Cold, sub-zero winter winds soon damage evergreen shrubs that are not fully hardy. Their leaves become unsightly, with dry and blackened edges. Insert five 1.5m (5ft) long pliable canes about 13cm (5in) deep into the compost around the tub's edge.

3 Starting from the top of the wigwam, spread a layer of straw evenly over the entire surface. (Alternatively, use hay, but this is not as weather resistant as straw.) Secure the end of a ball of string to the top and start winding downwards, in a slight spiral. Add more straw as the spiral proceeds.

2 Gently pull the tops of the canes together, so that they cross 15–20cm (6–8in) from the top. Use strong string to secure them together. If possible, flex the canes outwards, so that all of the plant's foliage is within the cage formed by them. If a few young and pliable shoots extend further outwards, this is not usually a problem as eventually they will be covered by a layer of straw.

4 Continue adding straw and forming a spiral of string. Add further straw until the bottom is reached, when the string from one circle can be tied to an earlier one. Tidy up and remove loose straw at the base. Throughout winter, regularly check the straw and remove it as soon as the weather improves. If left in position too long, the plant may be damaged in spring when growth resumes.

PLANTS IN LARGE POTS

The compost in large clay pots is easier to keep dry than that in tubs. All that is needed is to cut a piece of polythene to size, make a cut to its centre and to spread it over the compost. It is then quickly secured by a piece of string around the pot.

If possible, move plants in large pots into the shelter of a wall or hedge during winter. As a further precaution to them being blown over, secure some strong wire between two posts at a height of 90cm–1.2m (3–4ft), and tie the supporting cane in each pot to it. This technique is essential in exposed positions.

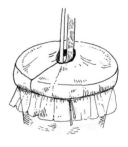

PLANTING POTS, URNS AND PLANTERS

These containers are filled with a wide range of plants, from ephemeral summer-flowering bedding types and spring displays formed of bulbs and biennials to herbaceous perennials which remain in a container for several seasons. Freely draining compost is essential to all plants, especially long-term types. Coarse drainage material in the base ensures water is able to escape freely and drainage holes do not become blocked.

In tall containers, added drainage can be created by inserting a narrow tube of wire netting down the middle and filling it with coarse drainage material. The area around it is then filled with moderately fertile, well-drained compost.

After a container has been planted with herbaceous perennials for several years, they become congested and have to be removed. At this time, empty all compost, plants and drainage material and thoroughly clean the container. Wooden types especially benefit from this treatment as any decayed timber can be replaced.

CHOOSING MATERIALS

A walk through a garden centre soon reveals a wide range of materials for pots, urns and planters. Be guided in your choice by looks as well as budget. Costly designs in lead or reconstituted stone often have inexpensive imitations. And you can always make square or rectangular wooden ones yourself.

CLAY POTS

Clay is a natural and traditional material and has the virtue of harmonizing with most plants. Also, it allows moisture to escape from the compost. It is cool during summer and keeps the compost warm in winter. There is a range of sizes.

GLASSFIBRE

This is increasingly popular and appears in a wide range of attractive finishes and colours, including sandstone, grey and white. Plain round, square and rectangular containers suit modern settings, or there are more ornate designs for a traditional look. All are strong, decay-proof and long-lived, but can be brittle if dropped or knocked. Glassfibre tends to warm up rapidly in summer and regular watering is essential to keep the compost moist.

PLANTING A HERB PLANTER

Good drainage is essential in containers. Often this can be achieved solely by forming a thick layer of pebbles in the container's base. But in a large herb planter, with an open top and cupped planting positions around its sides, it is better also to create a column of drainage material down its centre.

This is done by forming a piece of 12–18mm ($\frac{1}{2}$–$\frac{3}{4}$ in) mesh wire netting into a 7.5–10cm (3–4in) wide tube and inserting it into a planter with 2.5cm (1in) of pebbles in its base. Compost is then spread around it and plants put into the planting pockets, at the same time adding more compost. When the top is reached, fill this too with plants. Then water the compost thoroughly and regularly spray the outside with water until plants are established.

LEFT A planter packed with herbs makes a pleasing feature on a patio and is a practical one to have near a kitchen door. The textures, shapes and colours of their leaves provide many contrasts, and chives, thyme and sweet marjoram have pretty flowers. Other herbs to consider include parsley, chervil, lemon balm and young plants of fennel. These herbs are especially attractive when young and growing rapidly.

COLOUR AND SHAPE HARMONIES

Look at the textures and colours of planters, and try to choose ones that compliment the plants they contain. Natural stone is very versatile; the warm, earthy tone of terracotta makes a perfect foil for many plants; glazed containers in rich colours have a slightly exotic quality, well-suited to sculptural agaves and phormiums. Wood can be varnished or painted, perhaps in white or black, but some timber is left natural for a more rustic effect.

Some shapes seem to suit certain plants. Evergreen shrubs with rounded, bushy shapes look good in round tubs in natural materials, but an elegant agapanthus calls for something more sophisticated, such as a square planter of white or varnished wood.

ABOVE The false castor oil plant (*Fatsia japonica*), also known as the Japanese fatsia, Formosa rice-tree and paper plant, grows up to 6m (20ft) in its native Japan but in a pot or large tub it usually reaches no more than 2.4m (8ft) high. Choose a sheltered position for this plant. If it does exceed its allotted space, use sharp secateurs to cut back the offending stems to just above a leaf-joint in early summer, when there is no risk of frost.

WOOD

This is a versatile material, forming containers with a rounded outline, such as tubs and barrels, as well as square and rectangular planters. It is the nature of wooden containers to decay – and invariably this happens – but if made from strong, well-seasoned timber they last for many years. Because wood is in contact with damp compost this encourages decay, but if drainage holes in the container's base do not become clogged and there is at least 5cm (2in) of pebbles over them, this risk is reduced. Additionally well-drained compost is essential.

Always position wooden containers on bricks or broken pieces of paving stone, which helps to prevent drainage holes from becoming blocked. This also deters slugs and snails from attacking plants.

RECONSTITUTED STONE

This has a natural and mellow surface and can be formed into large containers, from dish and bowl-like structures to square and rectangular planters.

The thickness of this material helps to keep the compost cool in summer yet warm in winter. Containers are heavy and once in position need to be left there until emptied of compost.

Arundinaria viridistriata grows about 1.2m (4ft) high and is superb when planted in a pot and displayed on a patio. The slender purplish-green canes bear dark-green leaves striped rich yellow.

ABOVE Hostas are ideal for planting in containers. Some of these large-leaved plants are variegated, while others have all-green leaves, sometimes with a bluish sheen. Above is *Hosta sieboldiana*.

CLIMBERS IN POTS AND TUBS

Climbers growing in pots and tubs introduce a new dimension to patios. They cloak unsightly walls and create colourful backgrounds for other plants. Most have either beautiful and unusual flowers or handsome foliage; some have both. Some of these plants are annuals and each year are raised from seed, while others develop a permanent framework. A few have a herbaceous nature, dying down in winter to shoot again next spring and produce fresh stems and leaves.

All of these plants – and especially annual and herbaceous types – call for regular watering and feeding to support the vast amount of foliage produced each year.

Some of these climbers are fully hardy outdoors, while others, such as half-hardy annuals, are sown in gentle warmth in late winter or early spring and put outdoors when all risk of frost has passed in late spring or early summer.

ANNUAL CLIMBERS

These represent most of the climbers grown in containers. Some of them are hardy annuals when grown in borders, but for containers they need a rapid start in life and must be able to be planted into a container without too much root disturbance. Therefore, they are raised in small pots, earlier than normal.

° Perhaps the best known climbing plant is the sweet pea (*Lathyrus odoratus*), which can be grown as a hardy annual but is invariably raised in warmth in a greenhouse early in the year. The flowers are richly coloured, scented and ideal for cutting to decorate homes. Indeed, regular cutting ensures the development of further blooms. Provide plants with a trellis up which their tendrils will enable them to clamber. Dwarf varieties, such as 'Bijou Mixed', grow only 30cm (12in) or so high and are ideal in pots clustered around the bases of shrubs or other climbers, where they help to hide bare stems low down on plants. Such plants are especially useful.

° Morning glory (*Ipomoea tricolor*) is another well-known climber, growing 1.5–1.8m (5–8ft) high and producing large, trumpet-shaped flowers in blue, red-purple, or purple from mid-summer to the frosts of autumn. In a garden it grows 3m (10ft) high, but a pot diminishes its height to only about 1.5m (5ft). It is grown as a half-hardy annual.

° Nasturtiums (*Tropaeolum majus*) are hardy annuals, but when grown in containers raised as half-hardy annuals. While dwarf varieties are chosen for planting in hanging baskets, climbing ones do better when a trellis can be provided. The flowers appear throughout summer and into early autumn.

° Canary creeper (*Tropaeolum peregrinum*) is normally grown as a hardy annual, but for earlier plants raise it as a half-hardy annual. It is vigorous and in a garden may exceed 3.6m (12ft) high, but in a pot usually grows only to 1.8m (6ft) or less. From mid-summer to the frosts of autumn it reveals canary-

ABOVE The yellow-leaved hop (*Humulus lupulus* 'Aureus') is a spectacular herbaceous climber. It is usually grown to clothe arbours and trellises with large, golden-yellow leaves throughout summer, but it is also dramatic when planted in a large pot and trained over a wigwam of canes and wires. Water and feed the plant regularly during spring and summer.

yellow flowers. It can also be grown in a hanging basket or window box and allowed to trail.

* Black-eyed Susan (*Thunbergia alata*), a half-hardy annual, reveals a mass of white, yellow or orange flowers, usually with a black eye, throughout summer. Grow it in a large pot with canes to climb up to 1.2m (4ft) high. It is also suitable for growing in hanging baskets.

* Chilean glory flower (*Eccremocarpus scaber*), grown as a half-hardy annual, creates a mass of 2.5cm (1in) long, orange-scarlet, tubular flowers from early summer to the frosts of autumn. In a container it grows about 1.5m (5ft) high.

HERBACEOUS CLIMBERS

These persist in large containers for several years, but ensure that the compost in a large pot or tub does not dry out in summer, or freeze through excessive moisture in winter. Spread straw over the compost in winter.

* *Humulus lupulus* 'Aureus' (yellow-leaved hop) is the best known example. It grows 1.5–1.8m (5–6ft) high when planted in container, and from spring to autumn is covered in yellow, hop-like leaves. Form a pyramid of five strong canes to support the weight of leaves and twining stems. This climber forms a dramatic feature and produces a beacon of large, yellow leaves summer and into autumn.

LEFT This pretty *Bougainvillea glabra* is a very strong climber and the best species for growing in a pot as it will flower even when quite small. The plant needs to be positioned in a sunny garden or patio where it will be sheltered from the wind. The flowers themselves are small and white, but they are surrounded by beautiful purple bracts.

ABOVE The *Plumbago auriculata* is an evergreen flowering climber. This white-flowered species creates a pretty feature for the corner of a balcony, surrounded and enhanced by red busy Lizzies.

PERENNIAL CLIMBERS

There are many climbers that persist from one season to another, with a woody framework in some form. Clematis such as large-flowered types and the bushy Clematis macrocarpa form a mass of thin-stemmed shoots, while the Chinese wisteria (*Wisteria sinensis*) and *Prunus incisa* 'Kojo-no-mai' create a permanent, woody framework.

SHRUBS AND SMALL TREES IN TUBS

Evergreen conifers and both deciduous and evergreen shrubs and small trees create spectacular displays when planted in tubs. As well as creating focal points, they are features around which plants in small pots can be clustered, either for protection or for background colour. But do not congest them excessively and spoil their shape.

Planting a shrub in a tub is discussed on pages 70 and 71. Once planted, they need little attention, other than occasionally trimming off a misplaced shoot when flowering ceases. Additionally, every spring scrape off a 2.5–3.6cm (1–1½in) thick layer of soil from the compost's surface and replace it with fresh. Take care not to scrape too deeply and damage the shrub's roots.

If a plant is not fully hardy and likely to be damaged by exceptionally cold wind, wrap it with straw (*pages 72 and 73*). Also, ensure that the compost does not become excessively wet, causing roots to decay and the soil to freeze.

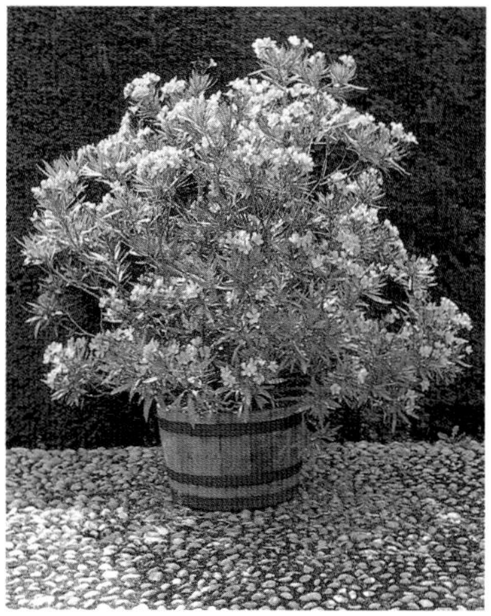

ABOVE Oleander (*Nerium oleander*) creates a dramatic feature in Mediterranean regions and other warm areas. It can also be grown in a tub or large pot in temperate regions, but does need to be given a sheltered position. In winter place it in a frost-proof greenhouse or conservatory.

Fragrant Shrubs for Tubs

* *Choisya ternata* (Mexican orange blossom): Sweetly scented orange-blossom-like spring flowers. The leaves, when crushed, smell like oranges. The variety 'Sundance' has yellow leaves and is smaller.
* *Lavandula angustifolia* (old English lavender): Lavender-scented flowers from mid-summer to autumn.
* *Mahonia* 'Charity': Sweetly fragrant, deep-yellow flowers from early to late winter.
* *Mahonia japonica*: Lily-of-the-valley scented lemon-yellow flowers from mid-winter to early spring.
* *Myrtus communis* (common myrtle): Balsam-scented white flowers throughout summer.
* *Nerium oleander*: The well-known oleander, with almond-scented white flowers during summer. It is only suitable outdoors in warm, sheltered areas. The entire plant is poisonous – take care.
* *Rosmarinus officinalis* (rosemary): Flowers mainly in spring, also intermittently throughout summer. Fragrant leaves.
* *Skimmia japonica* 'Fragrans': Lily-of-the-valley scented flowers during spring.

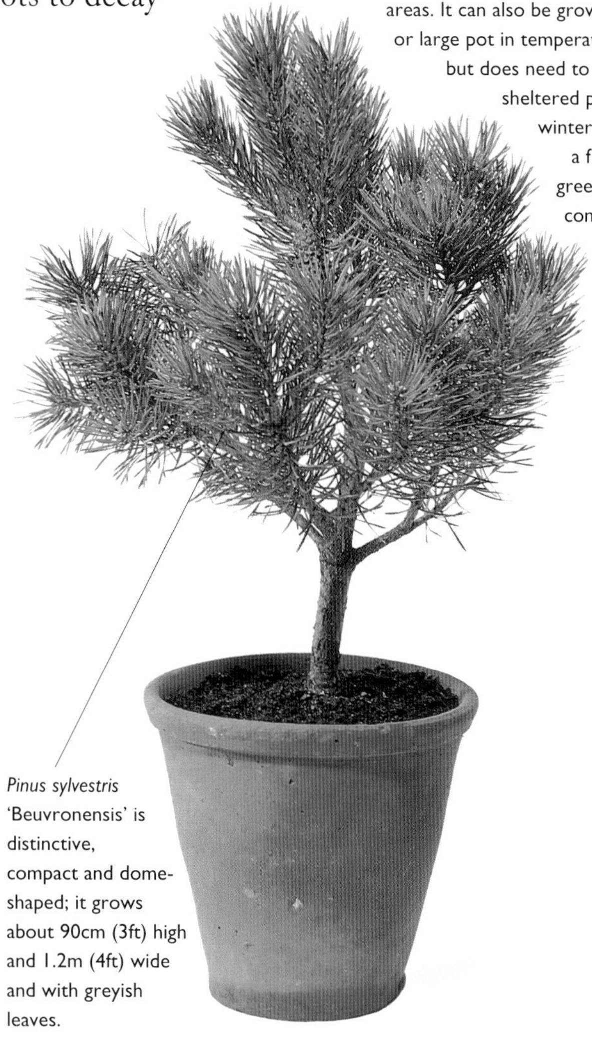

Pinus sylvestris 'Beuvronensis' is distinctive, compact and dome-shaped; it grows about 90cm (3ft) high and 1.2m (4ft) wide and with greyish leaves.

EVERGREEN SHRUBS AND TREES

Through their size and evergreen nature these shrubs create dominant features throughout the year. They range from the false castor oil plant (*Fatsia japonica*) with large, hand-like and glossy-green leaves to *Yucca filamentosa*, with spiky and somewhat sword-like, stiff leaves. Both are ideal in containers, but whereas the yucca's sun-loving nature and sculptural qualities make it look best positioned around formal swimming pools and underneath uninterrupted blue sky, the fatsia has an informal, jungly feel and needs a setting in light shade.

Camellias also need a light, high canopy of leaves, especially in late winter and spring. Their flowers are soon damaged when strong early-morning sunlight reaches them in frosty weather. A west facing position under an overhead balcony fulfils this requirement and enables camellias to be grown in tubs and large pots near buildings. The spotted laurel (*Aucuba japonica* 'Variegata') has a rounded shape; small plants can begin life as part of a winter display in a windowbox and later be put in a tub. It is hardy, but dry compost and cold winds cause leaf edges to blacken.

Other evergreen shrubs to consider include *Hebe × franciscana* 'Blue Gem', evergreen azaleas, *Buxus sempervirens* 'Suffruticosa' and *Phormium tenax*.

Deciduous shrubs include *Acer palmatum* 'Dissectum Atropurpureum', *Berberis thunbergii* 'Atropurpurea' and some rhododendrons. All of these plants are detailed on pages 95 to 107.

CONIFERS FOR TUBS

* *Juniperus communis* 'Depressa Aurea': Foliage golden-yellow when young.
* *Juniperus × media* 'Old Gold': Compact, with bronze-gold foliage throughout the year.
* *Juniperus squamata* 'Blue Star': Dense, silvery-blue foliage.
* *Pinus sylvestris* 'Beuvronensis': Compact and dome-shaped, with grey foliage.
(Further conifers are detailed on pages 95 to 107, together with their heights and spreads.)

ABOVE The Japanese maple *Acer palmatan* 'Dissectum' has low, bushy growth making it a good shrub for a tub.

Adam's needle (*Yucca filamentosa*) forms a spectacular, architectural plant in a pot or small tub and when positioned on a patio. In addition to the all-green form there is a variegated type with leaves edged in cream and yellow.

UNUSUAL CONTAINERS

To many gardeners, recycling old pieces of 'domesticana' to create an original design for a plant container is a challenge that cannot be denied. Unfortunately, the urge to personalize a garden often trespasses the narrow line between practicality and irrational, uncontrolled zeal. For success, the container must hold sufficient compost to support plants physically, provide nutrients and water, and be acclaimed as attractive.

Most unusual containers are suitable for summer only; it is only those that hold sufficient compost to protect dormant plants when temperatures plummet that are usable in winter. Nevertheless, summer is the season of bright colour, with perhaps a touch of seasonal silliness that should not be suffocated by too much tradition.

ABOVE Containers with 'funny faces' can be secured to a wall or fence and a pot of plants put in its top.

ABOVE This old, metal watering-can forms the centre-piece to this interesting arrangement of pot plants. The deep-red begonia is an eye-catching feature, while the trailing variegated ivies create the impression of cascading water.

IN SEARCH OF THE UNUSUAL

Granny's loft, car-boot and jumble sales, scrap yards and corners of a builder's yard often yield unusual containers. Most of these will be small and suitable only for summer-flowering bedding plants and spring-flowering bulbs. Nevertheless, they provide novelty; old chimney pots can be converted into plant holders (*page 93*), metal casks and barrels into miniature fish ponds (*pages 86 and 87*).

Old galvanized watering-cans, when painted and filled with summer flowers, are ideal containers, while war-time metal helmets turn hanging baskets into talking points. Even old, leaky rowing boats can be given a new life when packed with summer-flowering bedding plants. Large bird-cages also form eye-catching features.

An old birdcage filled with pot-grown summer-flowering annuals creates an unusual feature when suspended from a tree or a bracket on a patio. As the plants fade, they can be replaced by others. (Pot-grown chrysanthemums would follow on well.) Variegated, small-leaved ivies could be used to soften the edges of the cage.

Old clay drainage pipes can be used to create an unusual container. Traditional clay pipes are about 10cm (4in) wide and 30cm (1ft) long. Stand one pipe upright and cluster six others around it; use strong, galvanized wire to secure them together in three places. Then, bury them about 10cm (4in) deep in soil and fill with compost. Plant them with summer-flowering bedding plants; use trailing types around the edges. If this feature can be displayed in a sea of pea-shingle, it looks even more magnificent.

Old mop buckets with the dividing section removed form containers of a size well-suited to many plants. Drill drainage holes in the base, half fill with pea-shingle and stand plants – still in their pots – on it.

In rural areas, old milk churns are a possibility and form striking containers to display trailing plants. Painting them bright colours gives them even more emphasis: plant lobelia and nasturtiums around the edge, with a cascading fuchsia to add height in the centre. Water the compost regularly as it will dry rapidly.

READY-TO-BUY CONTAINERS

Some garden centres specialize in unusual containers and these include objects such as boots and shoes made of concrete, reconstituted stone or glass-fibre. These materials are also used to create tubs with smiling faces peering from a leafy surround.

Garden statues formed of concrete or reconstituted stone – perhaps depicting animals – can be used among containers created from similar materials. But do not mix synthetic and traditional materials.

OLD FOR NEW!

New terracotta pots have a bright appearance which after a few seasons dulls and becomes covered with a white patina. Instead of waiting for normal weathering, coat the surface with dilute cow manure or soot water, then place in a damp, shady position. Coating the surface with yoghurt also ages terracotta.

Old, metal baths make a very unusual but effective container for a simple but striking summer-flowering display of pansies, begonias, petunias, fuchsias and French marigolds. It is best to choose plants that are low-growing or trailing – but do not overfill the bath or the effect will be lost.

ROSES IN TUBS AND POTS

Planting roses in tubs and pots offers a way to grow roses even when only a balcony or small patio is available. Miniature roses are best in large pots and where a compost depth of at least 23cm (9in) is possible, whereas Patio roses are better in tubs and where a depth of 30cm (1ft) can be provided. Use a soil-based compost in the container.

Old boots can be used to display plants during summer. Cut drainage holes in the base, partly fill with drainage material and then add compost and plants. By cutting out planting positions in the toe areas, further plants can be added. Boots made from concrete and other materials are available, and these have a longer life than old shoes and boots.

STONE SINKS AND ALPINES

Shallow stone sinks planted with diminutive rock garden or alpine plants, miniature conifers and small bulbs become a feast of colour during spring and summer. Traditional old-fashioned cottage-type stone sinks are rare and costly, so look for the deep, white, glazed types that are discarded when older houses are being modernized. Modify the surface for a more natural-looking effect *(see below)*.

As an alternative to planting rock-garden plants, use half-hardy summer-flowering bedding types. If the sink is only slightly above the ground, choose upright and bushy plants. For a sink raised on a pier of cemented bricks, use trailing plants around the edges. For a superb display formed of just one type of plant, choose the African daisy *Osteospermum ecklonii prostratum* (earlier and still frequently known by gardeners as *Dimorphotheca*). It is lower-growing than the species and forms mats of large, white, daisy-like flowers during mid- and late summer.

DRAINAGE AND COMPOST

Good drainage is essential when growing plants in sinks. Unless the compost allows water to travel freely through it, the roots of plants soon decay, especially in winter. The base of the sink must have a layer of coarse drainage material to ensure excess moisture can escape. Filling a stone sink is detailed on the opposite page.

Most rock-garden plants thrive in a mixture of soil-based potting compost with extra sharp sand or grit. Where shallow, old, stone sinks are used, add further moist peat to enable the compost to retain moisture. When the sink is deep, this is not essential, as the greater volume of compost ensures that it does not dry rapidly. This especially applies to glazed sinks which have been converted *(see right)*. When lime-hating plants are chosen, devote a complete sink to them and use soil-based compost free from lime.

1 Old, white, glazed sinks can soon be converted into attractive patio features. After these sinks have been removed from kitchens and have sat outside for several months among building rubbish they are extremely dirty. The first step is to ensure the plug hole is not blocked. Then, use warm, soapy water to remove dirt and grease from the inside and outside. Thoroughly rinse with clean water. Use an old screwdriver or sharply pointed chisel to thoroughly scratch the sides and 7.5cm (3in) down from the rim on the inside.

2 Stand the sink on four strong bricks. These have a dual role: they keep the bottom edge off the ground while the sides are being coated, and later allow two strong timbers to be placed under the sink so that it can be easily moved and put in its display position. Use an old paintbrush to coat the sides and about 7.5cm (3in) down from the top of the inside with a PVA bonding glue. Ensure the surface is evenly covered. Wear an old glove to hold the brush to prevent hands becoming coated – the glue can be difficult to remove.

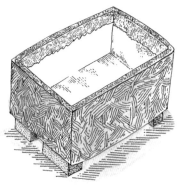

3 Mix and slightly moisten equal parts of cement powder, sharp sand and fine peat; form an even layer over the outside and about 7.5cm (3in) down from the rim on the inside. Allow this to dry slowly, as rapid drying encourages cracking. If the sink is in strong sunlight, place moist sacking over it. Before the coating fully hardens, use a trowel to round the edges.

FILLING A STONE SINK

Place a piece of perforated zinc over the plug hole, then a thin layer of broken clay pots over the entire base. Cover this with a 12mm (½in) layer of 6mm (¼in) pea-shingle and on this add 2.5cm (1in) of moist peat. Top up with compost (SEE LEFT) to within 2.5cm (1in) of the rim. When planting is complete, cover the surface with pea-shingle.

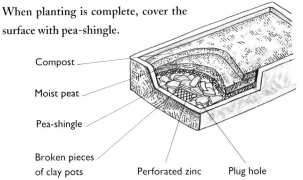

Compost

Moist peat

Pea-shingle

Broken pieces of clay pots

Perforated zinc   Plug hole

Stone sinks enable small rock-garden plants to be grown on patios and terraces. Raising the sink on bricks makes it easier to see, prevents the drainage hole from becoming blocked and reduces the chance of snails and slugs climbing and chewing plants. Elevating the sink on four piers of bricks cemented together makes it more accessible to gardeners in wheelchairs and easier to see. Ensure the brickwork is strong and the sink cannot fall.

BELOW A wide range of alpine plants, miniature conifers, small bulbs, dwarf shrubs and trailing evergreen plants can be grown in shallow stone sinks on a patio. A surface covering of gravel chippings highlights the plants and deters slugs and snails from climbing over the surface, and prevents large and heavy drops of rain from first hitting compost and then splashing earth on plants.

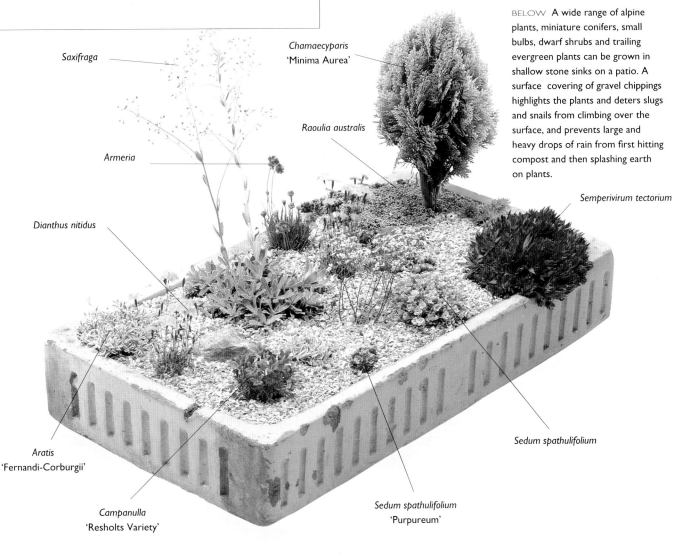

Saxifraga

Chamaecyparis 'Minima Aurea'

Armeria

Raoulia australis

Dianthus nitidus

Sempervivum tectorium

Aratis 'Fernandi-Corburgii'

Campanulla 'Resholts Variety'

Sedum spathulifolium 'Purpureum'

Sedum spathulifolium

BARRELS AND CASKS

Wooden barrels and casks have a traditional shape and rustic character that harmonizes with most plants and many settings. Large barrels, holding about 150 litres (40 gallons) are ideal as homes for strawberries, while casks are better suited for summer-flowering bedding plants; plants can be removed in autumn and casks cleaned and stored during winter. However, ensure that the wood does not become dry in storage, as it may shrink and distort and if this happens, the metal bands fall off and staves fall out. Traditional barrels were usually made from oak, although beech, elm, chestnut and spruce were also used. In addition to converting large barrels into homes for strawberries *(see below)*, they can be cut in half to form tubs or made into attractive rustic seats.

GROWING STRAWBERRIES

Strawberries grown in containers produce earlier crops than those grown in soil at ground level. Once planted, they can be left for five or so years before being replaced with young plants.

Drainage holes
Cleaning out the hole

1 Before drilling the barrel, thoroughly clean it. Check that the timbers are sound. Turn the barrel upside down and drill several 18–25mm (³⁄₄–1in) wide holes in the base to ensure good drainage. Use a chisel or coarse, round file to clean out the holes.

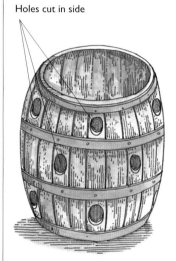

Holes cut in side

2 Between the top and bottom metal rings (each known as a chime) on a barrel, there are usually two other metal bands, each called a booge. Between these, drill a series of holes, into which strawberries can be planted. Use a drill, then a pad-saw, to make holes 5–6.5cm (2–2¹⁄₄in) wide and 15–20cm (6–8in) apart. Align the holes at the top and bottom and stagger the central row between them. Use sandpaper to smooth the edges of the holes and to rub down the wood and metal parts on the outside. Paint the metal parts black.

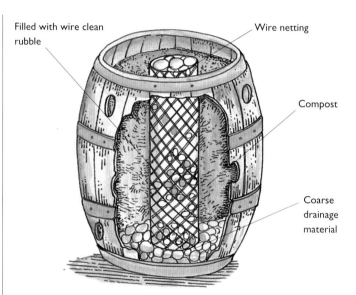

Filled with wire clean rubble
Wire netting
Compost
Coarse drainage material

3 Position the barrel on three or five strong bricks, so that it is level. Place large pieces of broken clay pots – concave side downwards – over the holes in the base. Add 10–15cm (4–6in) of coarse, clean drainage material, such as broken clay pots or pebbles.

Because the barrel is likely to be at least 60cm (2ft) wide and 90cm (3ft) high, the area of compost is large and special provision for drainage is essential. The easiest way to do this is to roll a piece of 2.5cm (1in) mesh wire netting to form a tube 10–13cm (4–5in) wide. Position the tube in the centre of the tub and fill with coarse drainage material. The tube's lower end rests on the drainage material in the base, with its top about 10cm (4in) below the barrel's rim. Start filling the barrel with compost or improved soil *(see page 71)*, at the same time planting a strawberry plant in each hole. Ensure the compost is firm. At the top, put in further plants, so that the barrel is covered. Water the compost and regularly syringe the plants until established. As the compost settles, it may be necessary to re-firm compost around the plants.

CAPTURING THE ATTENTION

Growing strawberries in barrels is not new, but it never fails to capture attention. The plants look pretty and the distinctive bouquet of the fruits as they ripen towards mid-summer brings an extra charm to patio displays. Apart from adapted barrels, proprietary plastic strawberry containers are available as well as earthenware pots with cupped holes in their sides. However, these do not hold as many plants as a barrel.

Barrels also make superb containers for displays of flowers and shrubs. Plants must be chosen carefully, however, to ensure they are not dominated by the heaviness of the wooden barrel.

BELOW Red, ripe strawberries tumbling out of a container are the epitome of a warm summer.

ABOVE Most flowers suitable for growing in containers can be grown in a barrel. This stunning display includes: yellow and orange French marigolds and mauve, purple and pink alyssum and lobelia.

LEFT Aucuba Japonica 'Variegata' makes a perfect plant for a winter barrel as it is at its best from autumn through to spring. It is a rounded, bushy shrub with gold-spotted, shiny, dark-green leaves. The female plant produces small clusters of bright-scarlet berries.

MINIATURE WATER GARDENS

Few features on patios create as much interest as ponds, and miniature water gardens can be formed from deep stone sinks, wooden tubs or large metal casks. The drawback with miniature ponds is the relatively small amount of water and its tendency to fluctuate in temperature throughout summer and to fall dramatically in autumn and winter.

The type of material used in a container's construction has a marked influence on its suitability. Wooden tubs are best, as water in them neither warms up dramatically nor becomes as cold as that in stone sinks and, especially, metal casks.

Miniature waterlilies and small marginal plants are essential. To keep them small and suitable for miniature water features they may need more frequent division than those in normal-sized ponds. Always put water plants in plastic-meshed planting baskets to enable them to be installed to the correct depth *(see below)* and removed for maintenance.

STONE SINKS

These make ideal miniature water gardens during summer, but in many areas the water is likely to freeze in winter. Where there is this risk, treat them mainly as summer features. Stand the sink on bricks to deter slugs and snails from crawling into it.

1 Wedge lightly crumpled wire netting in the plug hole and cover with concrete. Allow to dry, then thoroughly scrub the sink; use a hose pipe to rinse off soap and remnants of cement. If left, they contaminate the small volume of water in the sink. Choose a partially shaded position, but away from overhanging trees.

2 Position the sink on four strong bricks and ensure it is level and stable. Use a spirit-level. Evenly cover the base with a 2.5cm (1in) thick layer of well-washed 6mm (⅛in) pea-shingle.

3 Do not put water plants directly in soil in a container's base. Instead, always plant them in individual, plastic-mesh containers and stand on the pea-shingle. If leaves of

waterlilies cannot initially reach the surface, temporarily place the container on a brick. Suitable varieties are detailed on the opposite page. Also, use small marginal plants. These are also detailed on page 87.

A WATER GARDEN IN A TUB

Select a large, deep tub with strong, metal bands around it. Thoroughly clean it and fill with water to check for leaks. If it is not watertight, line it with a sheet of polythene. Fill with water and cut off surplus polythene level with the rim. Plant waterlilies and marginal plants in plastic-mesh containers.

TEMPERATURE EXCESSES

During summer, a miniature water garden can be placed in light shade to ensure the water temperature does not rise excessively. In winter, low temperatures are a problem. In areas where the temperature seldom falls below zero, little protection is needed. Just placing a sheet of glass over the container and securing it

by a string tied to bricks is sufficient *(above)*. Tying straw around it creates additional protection *(below)*, but once this becomes wet it has little insulating power. A large plastic bag packed with straw forms a more effective cover. In exceptionally cold areas, either empty the container and place the fish and plants in a large pond, or move it into a well-ventilated, unheated greenhouse.

MARGINAL PLANTS

These are aquatic plants that live with their roots submerged in water and most of their stems and leaves above the surface. The range of these for normal-size ponds is wide, but for miniature water gardens the choice is limited. Be prepared to divide them more frequently than in a garden pond to keep them well within bounds.

Plants to consider include:
* *Carex stricta* 'Bowles' Golden' (*C. elata* 'Aurea'): Grass-like, golden-yellow leaves. Height: 38cm (15in).
* *Iris laevigata* 'Variegata': Upright, sword-like green leaves with silver stripes and soft-blue flowers in early summer. Height: 45–50cm (18–20in).
* *Scirpus zebrinus*, also known as *S. tabernaemontani* 'Zebrinus' (zebra rush): Round stems banded in white and green. Height: 30–45cm (1–1½ft).
* *Typha minima*: Light-green leaves and flower heads during early and mid-summer. Height: 38–45cm (15–18in).

RIGHT Miniature water gardens are enhanced by fish, although they must be small and limited to about four. When introducing fish to a pond, do not just tip them in. Instead, lower the container holding them into the pond and allow the temperature to equalize before setting them free – sudden and dramatic changes in temperature will harm them.

MINIATURE WATERLILIES

Choose only the smallest varieties of *Nymphaea*. The recommended depth is that between the water's surface and the top of the compost in the container.

Varieties for water depths of 10–23cm (4–9in):
* 'Candida': White and free-flowering.
* 'Laydekeri Lilacea': Soft to deep rose.

Varieties for water depths of 15–20cm (5–12in):
* 'Caroliniana Nivea': White and fragrant.
* 'Ellisiana': Bright red and freely borne.
* 'Indiana': Apricot maturing to copper-orange.
* 'Paul Hariot': Pale yellow at first, later deepening to copper-red.
* 'Sioux': Buff-yellow, changing to peach.

WHEELBARROWS AND TYRES

Wheelbarrows, together with containers formed from car tyres stacked and secured to one another, create opportunities to individualize a garden. Displays in wheelbarrows are applauded by most gardeners, perhaps because they seem in context; containers formed from tyres are more controversial. But their utilitarian origins can be concealed to make robust, handsome large-scale tubs. The resulting containers have a degree of formality and a pair can look good positioned at either side of a garden bench. When painted white and packed with bright polyanthus in spring or busy Lizzies in summer, they are especially attractive. They look best when seen against the backdrop of a beech or yew hedge, with the deep green highlighting both the white tyres and the flowers.

By using large plastic buckets with holes in the base as inner containers, spring displays can be quickly removed and replaced with established summer-flowering ones.

PREPARING A WHEELBARROW

Old, wooden wheelbarrows can be given a second life when planted with a mass of bright-faced, summer bedding plants. Plant these barrows only for summer; empty them out and store them under cover in winter. Metal wheelbarrows can be used, but they lack the rustic character and the insulating properties of wood.

1 First, check the wheelbarrow to ensure it is sound and will support the weight of compost and plants. Reinforce or replace decayed timbers and use metal angle-brackets to secure wobbly legs to the framework. Then, drill several 12–18mm (½–¾in) wide holes in the base.

2 To prevent timbers in a wheelbarrow's base rapidly decaying when in contact with moist compost, line the inside with thick polythene sheeting. Where you drilled the holes in the base, puncture the polythene. Cover the base with about 5cm (2in) of pebbles or clean, coarse rubble to ensure excess water can drain. When this is in place, cut off the edges of the polythene level with the barrow's top.

3 Fill the barrow with well-drained but moisture-retentive compost, such as a loam-based type with extra peat. Evenly firm the compost and leave the surface about 2.5cm (1in) below the top. This allows sufficient watering space: when packed with plants and especially during mid- to late summer, it is essential that the compost is able to be thoroughly watered and to retain moisture without having to be watered every hour.

PLANTS FOR WHEELBARROWS

Use a medley of upright, cascading and trailing summer-flowering bedding plants. Plant a couple of larger plants in the centre, with a collar of cascading types and then trailing ones along the outside. Ensure that the top edge is well cloaked in flowers and foliage for a cornucopia effect.

Consider painting the wheelbarrow in a colour such as soft yellow, white or light green – or even in a combination – and choose flower colours that harmonize with their container. By echoing the paint colours of nearby woodwork, the display becomes co-ordinated with its background, too.

BELOW Wheelbarrows packed with summer-flowering plants create such eye-catching displays that they look good on their own. They are at their best when 'parked' towards a corner of a patio or to one side of a front entrance, as if they have just been wheeled there. (In fact, of course, they are impossible to move, and need to be planted in situ.) They need not be used completely on their own; in a group with pots and other small containers they look just as good, but they must be the dominant part of the display, in both size and colour.

FORMING A CONTAINER FROM TYRES

When painted white, car tyres stacked and secured to one another form an attractive feature. Choose tyres of a similar size (not too large), wash them and wire each one to its neighbour. Give them a coat or two of suitable paint. Place several bricks in the base and put a large plastic bucket (with drainage holes in its base) on top. Plant it with spring-flowering bulbs and wallflowers in autumn; use summer-flowering bedding plants in summer.

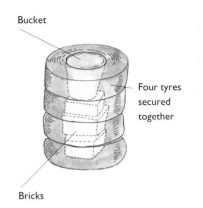

Bucket

Four tyres secured together

Bricks

ABOVE This traditional, wooden wheelbarrow is almost hidden amongst the foliage of surrounding plants. Using the same pretty flowers in pots as planted in the wheelbarrow gives the impression that this unusual container is about to be wheeled away.

MAKING A WINDOW BOX

Making a window box is not difficult, but does require sound timber, and accuracy when cutting the wood. Unless the measurements are uniform and correct, and the individual pieces cut with square edges and at right-angles, the box cannot be properly assembled and may soon collapse.

When deciding upon the size of a window box, first buy three equally-sized plastic troughs that can, in rotation, be put inside it. Never construct a window box longer than 90cm (3ft), as the weight of an inner plastic trough, moist compost and plants may cause it to break. If the window is wider than 90cm (3ft), make two short boxes to use side by side. Alternatively, use just one box and put cascading plants at the two edges to create the impression of additional width.

THE RIGHT SIZE

Choose an inner, plastic trough up to 75–90cm (2½–3ft) long and 20–23cm (8–9in) wide and deep. Use 18–25mm (¾–1in) thick timber for the box.

Cut the base 5cm (2in) longer and wider than the plastic trough, and the two long sides 5cm (2in) deeper than the trough and twice the thickness of the wood longer than the base. Cut the two ends to the width of the base and the depth of the sides.

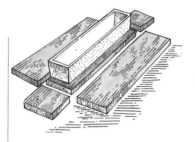
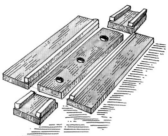

1 When all of the timbers have been cut, spread them out on a flat surface and position the plastic trough on the piece to be used as the base. It is then easy to check how they fit together and to see if adjustments to their lengths are needed.

2 Drill drainage holes in the base. Use 2.5cm (1in) square battens to secure the parts together. Cut and screw two battens – each 5cm (2in) less than the length – to the sides and the width of the wood from the edge. Also, fix battens to the ends.

4 When the box is assembled, coat the inside with bitumen paint to prevent rapid decay when wet. Also, paint the outside with a primer and couple of topcoats of a colour of your choice. The best colour is usually white, green or black.

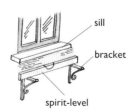

3 Begin by screwing the base to the sides. First drill holes in the base, about 12mm (½in) in from edge and 15cm (6in) apart. Coat the surfaces with waterproof glue. Use galvanized screws; they do not corrode and mark the wood. Drill holes, screw and glue the ends into position.

5 Cut four 2.5cm- (1in-) square battens of wood to fit across the inside of the box. Space them equally apart, screw in place and coat with bitumen. When dry, place the plastic trough in it. The small gap between the trough and window box will enable it to be removed.

BRIGHTENING CONSERVATORIES

The outsides of conservatories with brick walls up to about 90cm (3ft) high can be made more attractive by securing a series of window boxes to them. Position each box so that its top is a few inches below the base of the glass; the flowers can then be seen from inside as well. If the conservatory is fitted with windows that tilt outwards, position the boxes farther down the wall.

Summer-houses also benefit from window boxes, although because most windows in them are hinged either at the top or at the sides it means that the display has to be secured lower down on the building and cannot be seen from inside.

Where a window box is situated under a window and underneath a verandah or extended eave, frequent watering is essential during summer.

BELOW In spring window boxes and troughs can be magically awash with daffodils and polyanthus. To create a framework for these colourful plants, use a few small conifers and variegated trailing plants.

FURTHER USES

In addition to being used to create colourful window sills, window boxes can be secured to areas of wall between windows. If the space is between two windows on upper floors, secure the window box about 30cm (12in) below the boxes on either side. However, if the space is at ground level, position the wall-mounted box at the same height as the window boxes on either side.

For a more dominant feature between two windows, use two window boxes secured one above the other, about 38cm (15in) apart to leave room for trailing plants.

With all of these uses, ensure that the window box can be easily watered before fixing it in place.

ABOVE Window boxes and troughs need not be dull in winter. Small conifers, small-leaved evergreen ivies, winter cherries (*Solanum capsicastrum*) and winter-flowering ericas create colours throughout the season.

LEFT This rustic wooden window box contains a combination of summer-flowering and foliage plants, including French marigolds, busy Lizzies, fuchsia, variegated ivy, and white and deep-pink begonias.

USING GROWING-BAGS

Growing-bags are functional, versatile and offer instant homes to plants. They are unique in being both container and compost. The plants that will grow happily in them range from culinary produce to flowers. Tomatoes and lettuces are regularly grown, but not all vegetables are suitable. The relatively shallow depth of compost suits only those with fibrous or short roots. The bags are also ideal for low-growing herbs.

Spring-flowering bulbs are suitable, especially species and short-stemmed tulips and grape hyacinths (*Muscari armeniacum*), as well as self-supporting annuals for cutting and decorating a room. If positioned near the edge of a flat roof and filled with cascading bedding plants growing-bags can also create an attractive and relatively light weight edging.

Either two or four tomato plants can be planted in a growing-bag, depending on its size. But do not cram them in. Support for the plants is essential and these are illustrated below. Do not plant tomatoes until the weather is free from frost.

PREPARING A BAG

When stacked in garden centres and shops, peat-based compost in growing-bags becomes compressed. Therefore, the first task when preparing a bag is to shake it thoroughly, from both ends. Then place the bag in position on the ground or on a flat, pallet-like board and cut along the dotted lines to reveal areas of compost. Some growing-bags have a band that can be slipped over the centre to restrain the sides. Thoroughly water the compost several times before putting in plants.

RE USING BAGS

After a growing-bag has grown vegetables or flowers one year, it can be recycled for the following season. In the autumn, remove the plants and place the bag under cover. In spring, add a dusting of a general fertilizer, top up with compost and plant with summer-flowering bedding plants. For spring-flowering bulbs such as tulips and trumpet daffodils, remove the crop in autumn, top up with peat and plant immediately.

RIGHT As soon as the risk of late-spring frosts has passed, plant summer-flowering bedding plants in growing-bags. Use bushy plants in the middle, with cascading types at the sides to hide the bag.

Dwarf French beans in growing-bags do not need to be supported, but climbing forms must be given strong supports. Do not allow the compost in the bag to become dry.

SUPPORTING PLANTS IN GROWING-BAGS

If a growing-bag is on a pallet-like base or patio, a proprietary supporting framework is essential for tall plants such as cordon-type tomatoes and climbing beans. These rely on the weight of the bag to hold the base secure, with strong, supporting wires above it. Where a bag is on soil, long canes can be inserted into the compost, through the bag's base and into the soil. However, this does allow soil insects and diseases to enter compost in the bag.

A standard-sized growing-bag will hold eight to twelve lettuces. Sow seeds from mid-spring to early summer, or buy a few plants from a nursery or garden centre. Place the bag on a pallet; it helps to prevent slugs and snails reaching the plants.

CHIMNEY POTS AND WICKER BASKETS

The range of unusual containers for plants is wide and much depends on the imagination of gardeners. Traditional tall chimney pots are distinctive and can often be bought from specialist scrap yards. Old and weathered types generally blend in much better than new ones, although new ones can be rapidly aged by coating them with diluted cow manure for a few months to attract moss and lichen.

Wicker baskets are less weatherproof and better suited for plants left in their pots and displayed in lobbies and porches. Line the inside of the basket with polythene to protect it from excess moisture and pack moist peat around the pots to keep the compost cool and to reduce the frequency of watering the plants.

PREPARING A CHIMNEY POT

The outside of a pot can be left weathered and rustic, but remove soot and dirt from the inside. There are two ways to display plants in it. The easiest one is to wedge a plastic pot in the top and then put plants in it. Alternatively, fill the base with 36–50mm (1½–2in) of ready-mixed concrete, through which a 5cm (2in) long piece of 18–25mm (³⁄₄–1in) wide plastic tubing has been inserted to act as a drainage hole. When dry, add a layer of broken clay pots in the base and fill up with loam-based compost. Set plants directly in this.

Use a central, cascading plant, with trailing types around the rim to soften the outline of the pot.

An old, traditional, terracotta chimney pot, packed with small-leaved ivies and other variegated and all-green foliage, can make an interesting talking-piece. Choose your plants with care for this unusual container: it would be a mistake to use unsuitable tall plants or overfill it with trailing and cascading plants, losing the novelty of the container itself.

Ornamental wickerwork baskets can be used as containers for plants, especially in porches and lobbies where they will not become soaked with rain. Line a basket with polythene and then stand houseplants such as flaming Katy (*Kalanchoë blossfeldiana*) and chrysanthemums in it.

ORNAMENTAL PLANTS FOR CONTAINERS

The range of flowering and foliage plants that can be grown in containers is amazingly wide. Besides the plants suggested here, many other smaller shrubs, not-too-rampant climbers and even herbaceous perennials can be borrowed from the garden for permanent displays. But the mainstay of container gardening consists of plants grown for summer glory. Some of these plants are annuals - hardy or half-hardy, raised from seed each year and naturally dying off at the end of the growing season. Others are perennials in warmer climates but are treated as annuals in temperate zones - either discarded when autumnal frosts threaten or taken into shelter for the winter. Many of these are grown anew each year from cuttings, to create new, compact bedding plants.

In addition to the plants suggested and featured here, those for miniature water gardens are listed on pages 86 and 87 and for sink gardens on pages 82 and 83, and herbs are detailed on pages 66 and 67.

Abutilon pictum '**Thompsonii**', also known as *A. striatum* 'Thompsonii', grows into a lax deciduous shrub 1.2–1.5m (4–5ft) high and forms a handsome centre-piece in a tub. It is not hardy outdoors throughout the year in temperate countries. Its maple-like leaves are spotted yellow, and in summer it bears dangling orange flowers.

Acer palmatum '**Dissectum Atropurpureum**' is a hardy, deciduous shrub with a broad, umbrella-like outline about 1.5m (5ft) wide. This form has finely dissected, bronze-red leaves, while 'Dissectum' forms a green canopy. Both of them are especially attractive in spring. A large tub is essential.

Aegopodium podagraria '**Variegata**' (**variegated ground elder** or **variegated goutweed**) is a relative of the infamous and invasive ground elder. Though its variegation makes it less vigorous, it is safer to

A riot of purple and pink flowers tumble out of containers.

grow it only in a container. It can be exceptionally attractive, with light to mid-green leaves which are edged in white. It normally grows to be about 25cm (10in) high.

Agapanthus '**Headbourne Hybrids**' (**African lily**) are relatively hardy, clump-forming perennials with large, strap-like green leaves and umbrella-like heads with deep violet-blue to pale-blue flowers. They are borne on stiffly erect stems during mid- and late summer. They look especially good when planted in a square wooden planter. Protect the roots during the winter by covering the compost with straw.

Agapanthus '**Lilliput**', a diminutive African lily. It has narrow, mid-green leaves and stems topped with bright blue, trumpet-shaped flowers in umbrella-like heads. This flowers beautifully during the summer.

Agave americana (**century plant**), a succulent with spine-tipped, thick and fleshy grey-green leaves, is ideal in a large pot. In temperate regions, move it into the comfort of a frost-free greenhouse in autumn. The variegated form 'Variegata' is more attractive than the normal species and has yellow edges to the leaves.

Ageratum houstonianum (**floss flower**) grows 13–25cm (5–10in) high and develops masses of powder-puff-like flowers in white, pink, bright blue and mauve. Raise it as a half-hardy annual and plant in window boxes and troughs and at the edges of tubs.

Alchemilla mollis (**lady's mantle**) is a beautiful herbaceous perennial, with bright green, hairy, palm-like leaves surmounted from early to mid-summer with branched, wispy heads of yellow-green flowers. Plant it in a tub or large pot.

Anagallis linifolia '**Gentian Blue**' grows 15–23cm (6–9in) high and reveals rich-blue flowers with bright centres throughout summer. It loves to trail and is ideal for cascading over the front of a window box or hanging basket. It is a half-hardy perennial raised as a half-hardy annual.

Anthemis cupaniana is a cushion-forming herbaceous perennial, 15–30cm (6–12in) high and spreading to 30cm (12in) or more. During early and mid-summer it bears large, daisy-like flowers with yellow centres.

Antirrhinum majus (**snapdragon**) is raised as a half-hardy annual when grown in containers. Use low-growing varieties and plant in window

Ageratum 'Summit Blue'.

boxes and troughs, and around the sides of tubs.

Arundinaria viridistrata, a bamboo now known as *Pleioblastus auricomis*, is hardy, usually no more than 1.5m (5ft) high and ideal for growing in a large pot on a patio. This handsome bamboo has purplish-green canes and dark-green leaves, predominantly striped yellow.

Asarina purpusii '**Victoria Falls**' creates a tumbling mass of cerise-purple trumpets about 5cm (2in) long from early summer to the frosts of autumn. It is ideal for planting in hanging baskets, wall baskets and window boxes, where it can trail. It is a half-hardy perennial which is grown as a half-hardy annual.

Asparagus densiflorus '**Sprengeri**' (**emerald fern**), also known as *A. sprengeri* is mainly used as a houseplant in temperate countries. It has long, wiry, arching stems packed with green, needle-like leaves and in summer can be put in window boxes and hanging baskets. It is not a true fern.

Aucuba japonica '**Variegata**' (**spotted laurel or gold dust**) is a hardy evergreen shrub sometimes known as 'Maculata'. When young it is used to introduce colour into window boxes in winter and spring. It is also superb when planted in a large tub.

Begonia semperflorens (**wax begonia**) forms bushy plants 15–23cm (6–9in) high and

wide. It develops masses of red, pink or white flowers from early to late summer. It is a tender perennial widely grown as a half-hardy annual and planted into window boxes, troughs and the edges of tubs.

Begonia × *tuberhybrida*, a tuberous-rooted begonia, forms dramatic and eye-catching features in window boxes, wall baskets, troughs and tubs, or as a centre-piece in a hanging-basket. The flowers are single or double, often 13cm (5in) wide, and in colours including yellow, pink, red or scarlet from early to late summer. The form 'Pendula' (the basket begonia) trails luxuriantly and is ideal for planting in hanging baskets, wall baskets and at the sides of window boxes.

Bellis perennis (**common daisy**) is a hardy perennial usually grown as a biennial for planting in autumn in spring-flowering window boxes. It grows up to 10cm (4in) high and spreads to 13cm (5in). The white flowers are tinted in a range of pinks to crimson, and many are double.

Berberis thunbergii '**Atropurpureum**', a hardy deciduous shrub, has rich purple-red leaves throughout spring and summer. It requires a large tub, where it grows about 75cm (2½ft) high and 90cm (3ft) wide.

Bergenia cordifolia (**elephant's ear**) is a hardy perennial, mainly described as herbaceous but with large, rounded, dominant leaves that persist throughout winter. During the spring and the early summer, it develops clustered heads of bell-shaped and slightly drooping, lilac-rose flowers.

Terracotta and other clay containers flatter the plants.

It is ideal in a planter or small tub, where it grows about 30cm (12in) high and 38cm (15in) wide. The form 'Bressingham Ruby' is especially attractive, with glossy-green leaves that turn burnished maroon in winter.

Brachyscombe iberidifolia (**Swan River daisy**) grows about 38cm (15in) high with large, daisy-like flowers in colours including white, pink, blue, mauve and purple. 'Splendour', in both white and purple forms, grows 23–30cm (9–12in) high and is ideal for planting in a window box. It is grown as a half-hardy annual.

Buxus sempervirens '**Suffruticosa**', widely known as the edging box and usually no more than 25cm (10in) high in a container, has dark green, glossy leaves and is ideal for adding to window boxes in winter. It is also good grown in pots and clipped to shape.

Calceolaria × herbeohybrida (**slipper flower**) grows 20–30cm (8–12in) high, with pouch-like flowers in shades of yellow, red or orange and spotted in crimson. Outdoors it flowers during early and mid-summer. It is a tender perennial, raised from seed.

Calceolaria integrifolia (***C. rugosa***) is a half-hardy perennial raised as a half-hardy annual and planted into containers when all risk of frost has passed. The variety 'Sunshine' has bright yellow, pouch-like flowers from mid-summer to the frosts of autumn; it is ideal for planting in hanging baskets.

Calluna vulgaris (**heather or ling**) is a hardy evergreen shrub, with varieties ranging in height from 7.5cm (3in) to 60cm (2ft) or more. Their flowering period ranges from mid-summer to early winter, while many varieties are particularly grown for their coloured foliage. Choose low-growing varieties and use them especially in window boxes during winter.

Campanula carpatica '**Bellissimo**' grows to about 15cm (6in) and then trails. It develops chalice-shaped, blue or white flowers, throughout summer and is ideal for planting in hanging baskets and at the sides of window boxes. It is a hardy perennial raised as a half-hardy annual.

Campanula isophylla (**star of Bethlehem** or **Italian bellflower**) has a trailing habit and becomes drenched in blue bell-like flowers from mid- to late summer. There is also a white-flowered form. Use the Kristal varieties, as they can be raised from seed. Thus it is a slightly tender perennial, not hardy outdoors in temperate regions during winter. It is therefore best grown in hanging baskets in lobbies and porches throughout the year, and put outside in summer.

Centaurea cyanus '**Ultra Dwarf**' is a low-growing cornflower, 20–30cm (8–12in) high, with mounds of flowers in blue or mixed colours throughout summer. Do not use tall varieties in window box. It is a hardy annual but when raised for planting in containers is best grown as a half-hardy annual.

Chamaecyparis lawsoniana '**Aurea Densa**' is compact, slow-growing and densely packed with sprays of golden foliage. It is ideal for planting in window boxes in winter and tubs throughout the year.

Chamaecyparis lawsoniana '**Ellwoodii**' has dark-green foliage and a slow-growing, columnar nature. When young it is ideal for planting in window boxes in winter, as well as sink gardens throughout the year. When too large, transfer it to a tub or directly into a garden. For brighter coloured foliage

Buxus sempervirens 'Suffruticosa'.

Clematis montana 'Elizabeth'.

choose 'Ellwood's Golden' or 'Ellwood's Golden Pillar'.

Chamaecyparis pisifera 'Boulevard' is slow-growing and forms a cone shape packed with intense blue foliage. Plant young specimens in a window box during winter, later transfer to a tub.

Cheiranthus cheiri (wallflower), also known as *Erysimum cheiri*, is a hardy perennial invariably grown as a spring-flowering biennial. Use dwarf varieties for planting into window boxes in autumn.

Choisya ternata 'Sundance' is a slightly tender evergreen shrub with orange-blossom-like flowers in spring; its common name is Mexican orange blossom. If bruised, the yellowish leaves have the bouquet of oranges. In a tub it grows 1.2–1.5m (4–5ft) high and wide. Position in light shade and give protection from cold winter winds. Do not allow the compost to become dry.

Chrysanthemum frutescens (marguerite) has a sub-shrubby nature and grows 30–38cm (12–15in) high and wide. It is usually grown as an annual for planting in summer-bedding displays in borders and putting into window boxes and troughs. The white or pale yellow, daisy-like flowers appear throughout summer and into autumn. This species is now correctly known as *Argyranthemum frutescens*, but is invariably known and sold under its earlier name.

Pot chrysanthemums are sold throughout the year for decorating rooms indoors and when in flower last for a couple of months or more. They are also ideal for adding to window boxes and troughs outdoors, as well as putting in lobbies and porches. When their flower display is over, discard them and replace with others that are just starting to flower. They are not hardy and cannot be left outside in autumn or winter.

Clematis florida 'Sieboldii' creates a mass of passion-flower-like flowers during summer and into autumn. They are a mixture of white petals and violet-purple, petal-like stamens. It grows about 1.8m (6ft) high. Supporting canes are essential.

Clematis (large-flowered hybrids) are superb for planting in large pots or ornate planters. Plants are deciduous, can be left in position for several years and flower from early to late summer, depending on the variety. The colour range is wide.

Clematis macropetala grows up to 3.6m (12ft) when given a trellis to scale; it can also be planted in the top of a large barrel and allowed to cascade over the sides. During late spring and early summer it drenches the barrel with light- and dark-blue, nodding flowers up to 7.5cm (3in) wide. It is a perennial climber and can be left in position for several years, as it likes to become established.

Coleus blumei (flame nettle or painted nettle) is a tender foliage plant with colourful, nettle-like leaves. It is normally grown indoors in temperate climates, but in summer can be placed in window boxes and troughs. There are also trailing varieties, such as 'Molten Lava' and 'Scarlet Poncho', which are ideal for growing in hanging baskets.

Convolvulus tricolor, known as the dwarf morning glory and earlier as *C. minor*, is bushy and forms plants about 15cm (6in) high. The variety 'Ensign' has 5cm (2in) wide flowers from mid-summer to autumn, in blue, rose or white. It is a hardy annual, but when sown to flower in containers is best raised as a half-hardy annual.

Cotoneaster microphyllus-thymifolius is a hardy, dwarf, creeping and spreading shrub with narrow, dark-green glossy

Any corner can be filled with colour using containers.

Flowering container plants can be used to complement the colour of a window.

leaves. During autumn and winter it bears bright-scarlet berries. Plant in window boxes for winter display.

Crocus chrysanthus, about 7.5cm (3in) high, has golden-yellow flowers during late winter and spring. However, it is the hybrids that are mainly grown, in a range of colour mixtures including yellow, mauve, bronze, purple and white. These bulbs are ideal for planting in window boxes, troughs, tubs and sink gardens.

Datura meteloïdes **'Evening Fragrance'**, a half-hardy perennial grown as a half-hardy annual, has a bushy nature and is ideal for small tubs and large pots. It is now properly called *D. inoxia*, but invariably known by its earlier name. During mid-summer, 90cm (3ft) high and wide plants develop large, pure white, trumpet-shaped flowers. The foliage is slate-blue.

Diascia barberae **(twinspur)** is often acclaimed as one of the world's most beautiful annuals. It grows about 30cm (12in) high and is raised as a half-hardy annual. 'Rose Queen' reveals slender spikes of shell-like, rose-pink flowers throughout summer. When in containers, plant it about 15cm (6in) apart.

Dicentra 'Snowflakes' has delicately cut, mid-green leaves surmounted by clusters of pendulous white flowers from early to late summer. It is best planted in a large pot; a tub may overpower its intricately shaped and delicate flowers.

Dicentra spectabilis **(bleeding heart)** is a hardy herbaceous perennial, 45–60cm (1½–2ft) high and with rosy-red, heart-shaped flowers on arching stems during spring and early summer. It is ideal for planting in a small tub or planter.

Eccremocarpus scaber **(Chilean glory flower)** can only be grown outdoors in sunny, sheltered positions, when it is grown as a half-hardy annual. In a container it grows about 1.5m (5ft) high and develops masses of orange-scarlet, tubular flowers throughout summer and into autumn.

Epimediums **(barrenwort)** are ideal for tubs and large planters. The evergreen types are best, such as *E. perralderianum* and *E.*

pinnatum. They can be left in a container for six or more years before being removed and divided. Both of these species grow 23–30cm (9–12in) high and have yellow flowers in early summer.

Eranthis hyemalis **(winter aconite)** grows from tubers and produces lemon-yellow flowers with green ruffs during late winter and spring. The foliage disappears in summer.

Erica herbacea **(spring heather** or **snow heather)** is still better known under its earlier name *E. carnea*. It is a low-growing, hardy, evergreen shrub and from late autumn to late spring bears flowers in a wide colour range, including white, pink and rose-purple. It is ideal for planting in winter-flowering and spring-flowering window boxes or small types of containers.

Euonymus fortunei, earlier known as *E. radicans*, eventually forms a large, evergreen climber or creeping shrub, but the variegated forms are less invasive and when young are ideal for adding to window boxes and troughs, especially to brighten winter displays. Suitable varieties include 'Emerald 'n' Gold' (green and gold, with pink tinges) and 'Harlequin' (white and green). When these grow too large for containers, plant them into a garden.

Euonymus japonicus **'Microphyllus Variegatus'**, with variegated, evergreen leaves, has a diminutive stature and is ideal for brightening containers throughout the year, especially in winter and spring. It has small, green leaves with white edges, while *E. j.* 'Microphyllus Pulchellus' (or

A towering cascade of green and white.

Metal buckets make unusual but attractive plant containers.

'Microphyllus Aureus') has golden variegations.

***Festuca glauca* 'Blue Glow'** is an ornamental grass, ideal for growing in tubs and pots as it tolerates dry compost. It forms an attractive mound of spiky, silvery-green leaves. 'Sea Urchin' has bluish-green leaves. These grasses are perennials and can be left in a container for several years, before being removed, divided and replanted.

Fuchsias are popular as they introduce large splashes of shapely dangling flowers, often likened to tear-drops. Some varieties have a cascading habit, while others are bushy. Standards can make good centre-pieces for tubs. The range of varieties is wide, in many colours but all with dainty, pendulous flowers. The varieties grown in hanging baskets and other containers are not hardy outdoors throughout the year in temperate countries. Plants are raised from cuttings, grown during winter and put outside in early summer when all risk of frost has passed. It is best to buy established plants. A range of varieties is detailed on page 61.

***Galanthus nivalis* (common snowdrop)** is a diminutive bulb, 7.5–15cm (3–6in) high and with white flowers, marked green, during mid-winter and into spring. It is ideal for planting in a winter-flowering window box. The bulbs can be left in position for several years.

***Gaultheria procumbens* (partridge berry and winter green)** is an evergreen with a creeping and sprawling nature. It can be included in winter displays in window boxes, where it produces beautiful bright-red berries.

***Genista pilosa* 'Vancouver Gold'** is a hardy deciduous shrub with a mass of small, golden-yellow flowers during early and into mid-summer. When grown in a large pot it is 30–38cm (12–15in) high and spreads to about 1.2m (4ft).

***Glechoma hederacea* 'Variegata' (variegated ground ivy)** is an evergreen trailing perennial, ideal for planting in hanging baskets and window boxes. The stems hang for 1.2m (4ft) or more, displaying mid-green, kidney-shaped leaves with white markings. It also bears lilac-blue flowers in spring and early summer.

Godetia grandiflora forms a feast of funnel-shaped papery flowers from early to late summer. An annual, grown from seed, it has also been known as *G. amoena whitneyi*, but it is now properly classed as *Clarkia amoena*. Colours include white, pink, red and crimson on plants up to 38cm (15in) high. Choose dwarf varieties for window boxes in a wide range of colours.

***Hakonechloa macra* 'Albo-aurea'** is a hardy ornamental grass with a bushy and arching habit. It is ideal for planting in a tub or large pot, where it can remain for several years before becoming congested. The narrow leaves are vividly variegated buff and gold, with touches of bronze. It grows about 30cm (1ft) high before cascading.

***Hebe* × *andersonii* 'Variegata'** eventually forms an evergreen bush 75–90cm (2½–3ft) high and at that stage is ideal for growing in a tub. When young is better for planting in a pot about 23cm (9in) wide, where its green and cream leaves create an attractive feature on patios. From mid-summer to autumn it forms spikes of lavender flowers.

***Hebe* × *franciscana* 'Variegata'** is a compact, slightly tender evergreen shrub that is ideal for introducing additional colour to window boxes in winter. The leaves have cream edges and mauve-blue flowers appear intermittently throughout summer.

***Hebe pinguifolia* 'Pagei'**, also known as *H.* 'Pagei', is ideal

Fuschia 'Springtime' variety.

for brightening window boxes in winter. It grows about 20cm (8in) high and spreads to about 45cm (18in) when in a confined area and its small, glaucous evergreen leaves are accompanied by white flowers during late spring and early summer.

Hedera helix (**common ivy**) is a tough, trailing and climbing evergreen; it is the variegated forms that make the best contribution to containers. They introduce additional colour to winter and spring-flowering displays in window boxes.

Helichrysum petiolare (**liquorice plant**) is often sold under its earlier and more popular name *H. petiolatum*. It has cascading and arching stems packed with white, woolly hairs and rounded

silver-grey leaves and is ideal in hanging baskets. Raise it from cuttings taken in mid- to late summer; rooted plants are overwintered in a frost-proof greenhouse and planted in spring. A similar plant with smaller leaves is *Helichrysum microphyllum* (now renamed *Plecostachys serpyllifolia*).

Helichrysum petiolare 'Aureum', also known as 'Limelight', is similar to the grey species, but with soft yellowish leaves. Also, it is less vigorous.

Heliotropium × hybridum (**heliotrope**) a half-hardy perennial usually grown as a half-hardy annual, reveals fragrant, clustered forget-me-not flowers in rich-purple tones throughout summer and until the frosts of autumn. It grows 30–38cm (12–15in)

Unusual spaces can be brightened with bursts of colour.

high and the flowers have the fragrance of a cherry pie.

Helleborus orientalis (**Lenten rose**) is a hardy, evergreen perennial with dark-green leaves. During late winter and early spring it develops saucer-shaped, cream flowers. Additionally, there are pink, white, crimson and purple forms. Plants grow 45–50cm (18–20in) high in a large tub.

Heuchera sanguinea (**coralflower and alumroot**) is a hardy perennial with round, dark-green, evergreen leaves. However, the best varieties to seek are variegated types with a low-growing habit, such as 'Pewter Pot' and 'Snowstorm'. They are ideal in planters, tubs and large troughs.

Hostas (**plantain lily**) is a genus of popular hardy border perennials with attractively coloured leaves. They are also ideal for planting for summer interest in tubs. Many hostas are tall and striking, but it is the small ones that are most suited to planting in containers. Flowering is during mid-summer. Suitable examples include *H. crispula* (dark-green leaves with narrow, white edges and lilac-purple flowers); *H. sieboldiana*

(oval, mid-green leaves and white flowers tinged purple); *H.* 'Blue Moon' (deep-blue leaves and greyish-mauve flowers); 'Golden Prayers' (golden-yellow leaves and mauve flowers); 'Shade Fanfare' (green leaves with broad, cream edges); 'White Brim' (blue-green leaves irregularly edged in cream to golden yellow) and 'Zounds' (deeply puckered yellow leaves). Do not allow the compost to become dry, and position in light shade.

Humulus lupulus 'Aureus' (**yellow-leaved hop**) is a herbaceous climber and is ideal for planting in a large tub. Form a wigwam of supporting canes or allow the twining stems to climb up a trellis or fence behind the container. Large, yellow hop-like leaves drench the supports throughout summer. In cold areas, cover the compost with straw during winter.

Hyacinthus orientalis (**common hyacinth**) is usually represented in cultivation by the hybrid Dutch types. They are 15–23cm (6–9in) high and in containers outdoors flower in spring and early summer. Colours include white, pink,

The brilliant pink of a hyacinth.

blue and red. Position where their scent is appreciated.

Hydrangea macrophylla **(common hydrangea)**, a hardy, deciduous shrub, grows 90cm–1.2m (3–4ft) high and wide when planted in a large tub. Use slightly acid compost. Hortensia types with large, domed, flower heads from mid-summer to early autumn are the ones mainly grown in containers, but occasionally lace-cap types with flattened heads are planted.

Impatiens walleriana **(busy Lizzie)** creates masses of brilliant red, purple, orange, pink or brilliant white flowers on bushy plants about 25–23cm (6–9in) high throughout summer. Some varieties have a trailing habit and are ideal for hanging baskets, window boxes and wall baskets. Plants are raised as half-hardy annuals.

Ipomoea tricolor **(morning glory)** creates a feast of trumpet-shaped flowers in blue, red-purple or purple throughout summer and until the frosts of autumn. It is a twining climber grown from seed as a half-hardy annual and forms a screen up to 1.5m (5ft)

A garden border can be created with troughs.

high when in a container.

Iris danfordiae, a bulbous iris, is about 10cm (4in) high and during mid- and late winter bears scented yellow flowers. It is ideal in window boxes, troughs and sink gardens.

Iris reticulata, another bulbous iris, is 10–15cm (4–6in) high and during late winter and spring produces deep blue-purple flowers with orange blazes. It is ideal for planting in window boxes, troughs and sink gardens.

Juniperus communis **'Compressa'** is a slow-growing conifer, with a narrow, upright habit and grey-green evergreen foliage with a bluish tinge. When young it makes a good subject for planting in a window box during winter and spring, or in a sink garden.

Juniperus communis 'Depressa Aurea' is a low-growing evergreen conifer, ideal for planting in a large tub. When young, the foliage is golden yellow. In a tub it grows about 38cm (15in) high and spreads to about 90cm (3ft).

Juniperus horizontalis **'Wiltonii' (Wilton carpet juniper)** is slow-growing and

The bulbous *Iris reticulata*.

carpet-forming, with bright-blue foliage. It grows 15–20cm (6–8in) high and spreads to about 1m (3½ft). Plant it in a tub.

Juniperus squamata 'Meyeri' has an irregular shape, with arching and ascending branches to about 1.2m (4ft) or more and packed with steel-blue, needle-like leaves. It is ideal for planting in a large tub.

Juniperus scopulorum 'Skyrocket', also known as *J. virginiana* 'Skyrocket', is slow-growing and forms a narrow column up to 1.8m (6ft) high packed with silvery blue-green foliage. Plant it in a large pot or a tub.

Kochia scoparia **'Childsii'** is a compact and neat-looking form of the summer cypress. It is an annual, raised as a half-hardy annual and grown for its

attractive foliage. Use it as a centre-piece in tubs, window boxes and troughs.

Lathyrus odoratus **(sweetpea)** is a hardy annual climber raised from seed as a half-hardy annual for growing in a tub or pot. Plants are ideal for introducing a curtain of colour and fragrance to a trellis which acts as a background to other container-grown plants.

Lavandula angustifolia **(old English lavender)**, a hardy evergreen shrub, forms a mass of stems bearing narrow, silvery-grey leaves. From mid-summer to autumn it reveals spikes of pale, grey-blue flowers. A large tub is essential, as it forms a shrub 90cm (3ft) or more high and wide. *L.* 'Hidcote' is smaller, up to 60cm (2ft) high and wide and with deep purple-blue flowers.

A dull brick wall is easily cheered with colour.

Lilium **(lily)** is a large genus with many members that look good massed in pots, usually without companion plants of other kinds. There are several good candidates to choose from, including *Lilium auratum* (bowl-shaped, brilliant-white flowers with golden bands in late summer); *Lilium* 'Empress of China' (chalk-white flowers during mid- and late summer); *Lilium hansonii* (nodding, pale orange-yellow flowers with brown spots during mid-summer); and *Lilium speciosum* (bowl-shaped white flowers shaded crimson during late summer). Lilies vary in their cultivation requirements, so check that your site is suitable before you make your choice.

Linaria nevadensis **'Elfin Delight'** is a hardy perennial grown as a half-hardy annual when plants are needed for containers. Plants are bushy, about 15cm (6in) high and covered throughout summer with bicoloured flowers in yellow, orange, pink, lilac, flame, purple and violet. The flowers harmonize with the grey foliage.

Lobelia erinus **(trailing lobelia)** is well-known for its trailing stems packed with small flowers throughout summer. There are several varieties. Some forms make compact, bushy shapes; others have a cascading habit. The blues are classics (light, dark, with or without eyes) but other colours include white, lilac and crimson. They are ideal for planting at the edges of hanging baskets, wall baskets and window boxes. This half-hardy perennial is invariably grown as a half-hardy annual.

Lobularia maritima (earlier and better known as *Alyssum maritimum*) - sweet alyssum - makes a compact, colourful edging for containers. It is 7.5–15cm (3-6in) high, white, lilac or purple varieties in flower from early to late summer. It is a hardy annual raised as a half-hardy annual.

Lotus berthelotii **(parrot's beak, coral gem** and **winged pea)** is a tender perennial with long, trailing stems bearing slender silvery leaves. It looks good planted in hanging baskets, where the scarlet, pea-like flowers are clearly seen against the natural backdrop of their foliage.

Lysimachia nummularia **(moneywort** or **creeping Jenny)** is a hardy, creeping evergreen perennial with rounded, mid-green leaves and yellow flowers during early and mid-summer. It will carpet the surface and then trail from window boxes and wall baskets, as well as from troughs positioned on the floors of balconies or steps.

Lysimachia nummularia 'Aurea' is similar, but slightly less vigorous and with golden-yellow leaves.

Mahonia **'Charity'** is a hardy evergreen shrub eventually 1.8m (6ft) or more high when planted in a large tub. From early to late winter it bears deep-yellow flowers.

Mahonia japonica eventually forms a large, glossy-leaved evergreen shrub when planted in a garden. In a tub it can be kept at 1.5m (5ft) or less. From early to late winter it develops spikes of fragrant, lemon-yellow flowers.

Hanging plants trail gently downwards.

Narcissus 'Tête à Tête'.

Mesembryanthemum criniflorum (Livingstone daisy) is a half-hardy perennial raised as a half-hardy annual in gentle warmth in a greenhouse in late winter or early spring. Plant it in a window box, trough or large, dish-like container as soon as all risk of frost has passed. The succulent leaves are light green, and the daisy-like flowers appear in a wide range of brilliant colours throughout summer. Plants grow 10–15cm (4–5in) high and create a mat of colour.

Mimulus 'Malibu Orange' (monkey flower) grows 13–15cm (5–6in) high and produces a dazzling display of orange flowers. Other varieties have mixed colours, including cream, red and golden-orange. It is raised as a half-hardy annual plant.

Muscari armeniacum (grape hyacinth) is a bulb and once planted in a container can be left alone to flower each spring. It has blue flowers about 15cm (6in) high. When plants become congested – usually after three or four years – remove them, divide and replant them.

Myosotis sylvatica (forget-me-not) is a hardy biennial planted into spring-flowering window boxes and tubs in autumn. The misty-blue flowers are ideal for combining with tulips.

Myrtus communis (common myrtle) is a slightly tender evergreen shrub best grown in a pot placed outdoors in summer and in a conservatory or greenhouse during winter. Fragrant, white, saucer-shaped flowers about 2.5cm (1in) wide appear throughout summer.

Narcissus bulbocodium (hoop-petticoat daffodil), a miniature bulb about 15cm (6in) high, develops somewhat cone-shaped, yellow trumpets during late winter and early spring. It is ideal for planting in sink gardens and winter-flowering displays in window boxes.

Narcissus cyclamineus, a diminutive bulb about 15cm (6in) high, is ideal for planting in a sink garden and winter-flowering displays in window boxes. The slightly pendent, late winter and early spring flowers, are about 5cm (2in) long, with small trumpets and petals that sweep backwards.

Narcissus triandrus 'Albus' is a miniature bulb with drooping, creamy-white flowers during early and mid-spring. It is ideal for planting in sink gardens.

Narcissus with trumpets are widely known as daffodils. They are ideal for planting in spring-flowering displays in window boxes, troughs and tubs. Choose short varieties for planting in window boxes and other exposed positions, whereas taller ones can be put in tubs.

Nemophila maculata '5-Spot' grows 7.5–15cm (3–6in) high, then trailing. Each of the five light-blue petals has a deep-blue spot at its tip. Grow it as a half-hardy annual.

Nemophila menziesii 'Pennie Black' is 5–10cm (2–4in) high, then spreads widely. The purple to black flowers have scalloped, white edges, and appear throughout summer. Grow it as a half-hardy annual.

Nerium oleander (oleander), a Mediterranean shrub, is a slightly tender evergreen shrub in temperate countries and therefore best grown in a large pot positioned outdoors in

The yellow in this brilliant spring display seems to jump out of the containers.

summer but brought in to a greenhouse or conservatory during winter. In summer it bears scented white flowers. Ensure that no part of the plant is eaten or chewed.

Nicotiana alata **(tobacco plant)** has sweetly scented flowers in a range of colours throughout summer. Many varieties are 90cm (3ft) high, but choose shorter types at 25–30cm (10–12in) high to brighten window boxes, troughs and tubs. Raise plants as half-hardy annuals.

Nierembergia **'Mont Blanc'** grows 10–15cm (4–6in) high and creates a feast of cup-shaped, white flowers throughout summer. It is a half-hardy perennial best raised as a half-hardy annual.

Osteospermum ecklonis prostratum **(African daisy)** was earlier known as *Dimorphotheca ecklonis* 'Prostratam'. These perennials are raised as half-hardy annuals and are ideal for planting in tubs, window boxes and raised sinks totally devoted to them. It creates a wealth of large, daisy-like, white flowers during summer.

Pelargonium × *hortorum* **(zonal pelargonium)** covers a wide range of upright growing tender perennials once known as geraniums. The rounded leaves often have bronze or maroon markings. The range of varieties is wide, with flowers in red, crimson, salmon-pink and white throughout summer. There are dwarf varieties only 13cm (5in) high, so you can scale plants to suit the size of your container. They all grow well in relatively small pots.

Pelargonium peltatum **(ivy-leaved geranium)** is grown for

Nicotiana, the tobacco plant, sweetly scents the air.

its trailing habit. The mid-green fleshy leaves resemble the shape of the common ivy, and flowers in a wide colour range appear in umbrella-like heads from early summer to the frosts of autumn. They are ideal for planting in window boxes, hanging baskets and wall baskets, their shapely foliage is well-displayed.

Cascade geraniums, also known as Balcon and Continental geraniums, sprawl and tumble,

like the ivy-leafed geraniums from which they are derived. They produce masses of flowers throughout the summer. Varieties come in shades of pink, lilac, salmon and scarlet. Buy established plants each year, plant them close together and do not excessively feed them.

Petunia × *hybrida* **(garden petunia)** creates a magnificent display of trumpet-shaped velvet-textured flowers

throughout summer in single or mixed colours, in shades of white, blue, pink, blush, cerise, violet and scarlet. Some types can be bushy, while others are cascading. Raise new plants as half-hardy annuals.

Phormium tenax **(New Zealand flax** or **New Zealand hemp)** is an evergreen perennial only half-hardy in temperate regions. It therefore needs coddling, such as in a wind-protected, sunny corner and a large container like a tub. Place straw over the compost in winter. It is a handsome plant, with wide, leathery, strap-like, deep-green leaves. When planted in borders, phormiums become striking specimens often 3m (10ft) high, but in tubs they grow to 1.5m (5ft) or less, especially if coloured-leaved and variegated forms such as 'Purpureum' (bronze-purple) and 'Variegatum' (striped green and yellow) are planted. There are many other varieties from which to choose.

Pinus sylvestris **'Beuvronensis'** is a dwarf form of the Scots pine. It grows 60–75cm (2–2½ft) high and spreads to 1m (3½ft), with branches packed with grey-green needles. It is especially attractive in spring. Plant it in a tub.

Polygonum affine **'Donald Lowndes'** is a hardy herbaceous perennial, now properly known as *Persicaria affine* 'Donald Lownes' but invariably sold under its earlier name. It has a compact habit and forms a mat of bright-green leaves when young. During early summer it develops rosy-red flower spikes. It is ideal for planters, tubs and large troughs.

Primula auricula (**auricula**), an alpine primula, is the parent of many varieties in colours including yellow, red and blue. The 15cm (6in) high plants are characterized by the primrose-shaped flowers with circular zones of colour during spring.

Primula polyantha, the well-known polyanthus which creates masses of colourful flowers during spring and early summer is raised as a hardy perennial. It is a hybrid between the primrose *(P. vulgaris)* and cowslip *(P. veris)*. Plants grow 15–20cm (6–8in) high and are ideal for planting in tubs, window boxes and troughs.

Prunus incisa 'Kojo-no-mai' (sometimes written 'Kojo nomai') is superb when planted in a large, wide pot or tub. It grows about 1.2m (4ft) high and 3–3.6m (10–12ft wide), with red-centred pink flowers that fade to white in spring, glorious autumnal-coloured leaves before falling, then an intricate arrangement of shoots that when highlighted by frost create a further spectacle.

Rosmarinus officinalis (**rosemary**) is a hardy evergreen shrub with aromatic, dark-green, needle-like eaves with white undersides. Small, mauve flowers are mainly borne in spring, also intermittently throughout the rest of summer. When growing in a large tub, plant seven or more small cuttings and during the first two years regularly pinch out their growing tips to encourage bushiness.

Salvia splendens (**scarlet salvia**) grows 20–25cm (8–10in) high and creates a galaxy of flowers throughout summer. There is a range of varieties, with flowers in scarlet, as well as purple, salmon and white. They are ideal for planting in troughs, window boxes and tubs. Raise new plants as half-hardy annuals.

Sedum spectabile (**ice plant**) is a hardy perennial with thick, grey-green leaves. Its clustered heads of pink flowers during late summer and autumn add interest to small tubs.

Sempervivum tectorum (**common houseleek**), a hardy rosette-forming evergreen succulent, is ideal for planting in pots and unusual containers. Plants spread to carpet the surface with an intriguingly textured mass of leaves, softened by flower spikes in summer. The variety 'Commander Hay' is especially charming with its richly coloured leaves.

Senecio bicolor (cineraria or *S. cineraria)*, earlier known as *S. maritimus and Cineraria maritima*, is a beautiful silver-leaved plant that is ideal for planting in window boxes. The form 'Silver Dust' has bright, silvery-white, fern-like leaves. A half-hardy perennial, it is best grown outdoors only, in summer, but does survive low temperatures in mild winters. For compact, healthy plants, grow from cuttings each year.

Senecio × hybridus bears the daisy-like flowers commonly known as cinerarias (previous botanical names were *Cineraria cruenta* and *Seneccio cruentus*). It is a half-hardy perennial usually grown as a perennial.

Silene pendula '**Peach Blossom**' is only 10–15cm (4–6in) high, with a branching and spreading habit that enables it to saturate hanging baskets and window boxes with colour throughout summer. The deep-pink flower buds open to salmon, then white. It is a hardy annual, but when grown in containers is best raised as a half-hardy annual.

Skimmia Japonica '**Fragrans**' is a hardy evergreen shrub that can be grown in a large tub, where it becomes about 90cm (3ft) high and wide. Scented flowers appear in spring.

Skimmia japonica '**Rubella**' is a hardy evergreen shrub with clusters of bright-red flower buds throughout winter. In spring these buds open to white flowers revealing yellow anthers. It is ideal for introducing colour to window boxes in winter.

Stachys byzantina (also known as *S. olympica* and *S. lanata*), is widely called lamb's tongue and forms an attractive feature

Polyanthus, a primrose hybrid.

in a tub or large pot. It grows up to 38cm (15in) high and spreads to about 45cm (18in), with oval leaves smothered in soft, furry, silvery hairs. For the best foliage, choose the non-flowering variety 'Silver Carpet'.

***Tagetes patula* (French marigold)** develops yellow flowers throughout summer. They are raised as half-hardy annuals; the low-growing forms are the ones to choose for compact displays. Other marigolds can be used, but ensure they are dwarf.

Taxus baccata* *'Standishii' forms a narrow column packed with old-gold foliage. It is a slow-growing yew and even after ten years may be only 75cm (2½ft) high. Plant it first in a large pot, later a tub.

***Thuja orientalis* 'Aurea Nana'** has a bun-like shape, packed with near vertical, flattened sprays of bright golden-yellow foliage. In autumn, the tips become golden. When young, it is ideal in a window box in winter; later plant it into a large pot or tub.

***Thunbergia alata* (black-eyed Susan)**, a half-hardy twining climber usually grown from seed as an annual, is famed for its white, yellow or orange flowers, each with a dominant black centre. They are borne throughout summer on plants up to 1.2m (4ft) high. This can also be grown in hanging baskets: pinch out the tips to encourage a mass of sprawling stems.

***Tolmiea menziesii* (pig-a-back plant or youth-on-age)** is an evergreen perennial grown for its mound of pale green maple-like leaves. It is hardy enough to grow outdoors in temperate climates as well as indoors in cool rooms. It is also ideal for planting in hanging baskets and other containers in lobbies.

Black-eyed Susan, a pretty, hardy climber.

Young plantlets form on mature leaves, hence the common names.

Tradescantia fluminensis is a well-known trailing houseplant, sufficiently hardy to be used in porches and lobbies. In warm areas it can also be planted in hanging baskets outdoors. The long, trailing stems are peppered with pointed variegated leaves.

***Tropaeolum majus* 'Double Gleam Mixed'**, a trailing nasturtium, produces semi-double, scented flowers in yellow, orange and scarlet. Sow seeds in pots and plant into containers as soon as all risk of frost has passed.
When grown in a large pot or tub, it can also be grown to cover a screen about 1.8m (6ft) high.

***Tropaeolum peregrinum* (canary creeper)** is grown as a half-hardy annual twining climber when planted in a container. In a pot it seldom grows more than 1.8m (6ft) high and develops frilled canary-yellow flowers through summer and into autumn, among rounded bright-green leaves.

Tulipa fosteriana, a bulbous plant, grows 30–38cm (12–15in) high and reveals wide, scarlet tulip flowers during mid-spring. Plant the bulbs in tubs in autumn.

Tulipa greigii, grows 23–30cm (9–12in) high and produces orange-scarlet flowers about 7.5cm (3in) long during mid-spring. The flowers are borne amid grey-green leaves veined or marbled in bronze or purple-brown. Its low stature makes it ideal for planting in spring-flowering window boxes, as well as tubs.

There are many varieties derived from this species, in colours which include both yellow and red.

Tagetes patula, the French marigold.

Tulipa kaufmanniana **(waterlily tulip)** grows up to 25cm (10in) high and develops large white flowers flushed with red and yellow on the outside during early and mid-spring. There are many hybrids, in colours including yellow and red, salmon-pink, white, cream and red, red and yellow. Plant it in window boxes and tubs.

Many other tulips are popular in tubs and window boxes in spring; it is essential to choose low-growing varieties of Single Early and Double Early types for containers in exposed positions.

Ursinia anethoides is a half-hardy perennial raised as a half-hardy annual. It grows 23–38cm (9–15in) high, spreads to about 25cm (10in) and bears large, daisy-like flowers with bright orange-yellow centres from early to late summer.

Venidium fastuosum **(monarch of the veldt)** is raised as a half-hardy annual, when it grows about 50cm (20in) high. The woolly leaves are deeply cut, with large, orange flowers with black-purple centres throughout summer. It is ideal when planted in a large pot.

Verbena × *hybrida* **(vervain)** has several short and trailing varieties that are perfect for planting in hanging baskets or window boxes. They create domed heads packed with flowers. Colours include white, carmine, blue, mauve and scarlet. This half-hardy perennial is invariably raised as a half-hardy annual.

Vinca minor **'Variegata'**, the variegated lesser periwinkle, creates masses of trailing and sprawling stems packed with green and creamy-white variegated leaves. It is hardy and ideal for adding to winter displays in hanging baskets or

An interesting variety of colours and shapes.

for permanent planting in tubs. When too large for a container, replant it in a garden.

Viola × *wittrockiana* **(garden pansy)** has large-faced long-lasting flowers in mixed and single colours. There are both winter- and summer-flowering varieties, while flowers can also be produced in spring by selecting early-flowering types. There are many varieties and they are widely available as established plants.

Wisteria sinensis **(Chinese wisteria)** is a hardy climber usually trained against a wall; it can also be grown in a large, wide pot or tub and pruned and trained to create a self-supporting framework of branches. Fragrant, pendulous clusters of mauve flowers appear during late spring and early summer.

Yucca filamentosa has a clinical outline, with stiff, somewhat

sword-like evergreen leaves that arise like a large rosette. Plant it to make a dramatic specimen in a large tub. The smaller form, *'Variegata'*, is much more attractive, with broad, cream edges to the leaves.

Zebrina pendula **(silvery inch plant)** is grown as a houseplant in temperate countries and is sufficiently hardy to be put in hanging baskets in lobbies and porches. In warm areas it can also be put in hanging baskets outside. The trailing stems bear green leaves with broad, silvery areas along the outside. Correctly, this plant is now known as *Tradescantia zebrina*, but it is invariably sold under its old name.

Zinnia elegans **(youth-and-old-age)** is a half-hardy annual that creates a mass of large, colourful dahlia-like flowers from mid-summer to the frosts of autumn. Choose dwarf strains for planting in pots.

Viola x *wittrockiana*, Jolly Joker.

GLOSSARY

Alpine A plant native to zones officinally classified as being between the upper limits of trees and the permanent snow line. Alpine plants can be grown in miniature gardens in shallow stone sinks.

Annual A plant that is raised from seed and completes its life-cycle within one growing season. Some annuals are half-hardy in temperate zones and raised in gentle warmth in late winter or early spring. They are planted into containers in late spring and early summer, as soon as the risk of frost has passed.

Barrels Wooden containers earlier used to transport all manner of goods including beer, flour, tobacco and gunpowder. They ranged from a pin (20 litres/4$\frac{1}{2}$ gallons) to a butt (490 litres/108 gallons). Today, medium to large barrels are either cut in half to form tubs, or left intact and drilled along their sides and base

and used to display flowers orgrow strawberries.

Biennial A plant that takes two season to grow from seed and to produce flowers. Many spring-flowering plants grown in containers are biennial, such as daisies and wallflowers.

Bulb Formed of overlapping, fleshy, modified leaves, creating a food-storage organ that, when given the right conditions, develops leaves and flowers. Many spring-flowering plants in containers are bulbs, such as hyacinths and daffodils.

Centre-pieces Plants put in the centres of displays to create dominant features. In hanging-baskets, cascading fuchsias are frequently used for this purpose.

Coade stone Terracotta-type, artificial stone made during the late 1700s and early 1800s. Containers made of this material are highly prized.

Coir-based compost A new type of compost that does not include peat or loam and

therefore is termed environmentally friendly.

Compost additives Materials - such as Vermiculite and Perlite - added to composts to enable them to retain extra moisture.

Courtyards Originally, open areas surrounded by buildings or walls, perhaps inside a castle. Nowadays, they are usually paved areas at the rear of a building and surrounded by a wall.

Crocks: Pieces of broken clay pots used to cover drainage holes in containers. They are placed concave side downwards.

Dead-heading The removal of faded flowers to encourage the development of further blooms.

Deciduous Trees and shrubs that shed their leaves in autumn and develop fresh ones during the following spring.

Drip-tray Integral with plastic-type hanging-baskets to prevent water dripping on floors or paths beneath

them. They are usually used in lobbies and porches.

Evergreen Trees and shrubs that appear to retain their leaves throughout the year, although continually some are being shed while fresh ones formed.

Foam-liner Used to help retain moisture in hanging-baskets.

Frost-tender Plants that are killed or seriously damaged by frost.

Growing-bag Originally introduced to grow tomatoes on disease-infected soil, but now widely used as homes for many flowering and food crops.

Hardening off The gradually acclimatizing of plants raised in gentle warmth in a greenhouse to outdoor conditions. Half-hardy summer-flowering bedding plants are treated in this way.

Herbaceous perennials Plants that die down to soil-level in autumn and send up fresh shoots in spring. Some of these plants can be grown in tubs and other large containers.

Jardiniere A large, decorative stand or pot that is used to display plants.

John Innes composts Loam-based compost, originated during the 1930s at the John Innes Horticultural Institute, Britain. They standardized composts for sowing seeds and potting and repotting plants.

Loam-based compost Compost formed mainly of fertile topsoil with the addition of sharp sand, peat and fertilizers.

Manger Similar to wire-framed wall-baskets, but with a wider metal framework.

Patio The Spaniards used this term to describe an inner court, open to the sky and surrounded by a building. The term was introduced by Spaniards to North America where it came to mean any paved area around a dwelling.

Peat-based compost Compost formed mainly of peat, with the addition of fertilizers.

Perlite A moisture-retentive material added to compost.

Reconstituted stone Used to construct a wide range of

plant containers and ornaments. It mellows to a pleasing colour.

Re-used growing-bags Growing-bags which have been used for one season can be topped up with fresh peat and fertilizers and used to grow summer-flowering bedding plants.

Shrub A woody plant with several stems arising from ground-level.

Sink gardens A way to grow small plants such as miniature conifers, alpine plants and bulbs. Stone sinks are best, but modified glazed types can also be used.

Sphagnum moss A type of moss, earlier and widely used to line wire-framed hanging-baskets to assist in moisture-retention, retain compost within the container and to create a attractive feature. Nowadays, it has been almost totally replaced by the use of black plastic.

Spring-flowering bedding plants These are usually biennials which are planted into containers in late summer or autumn for flowering in spring and early summer. They are often combined with spring-flowering bulbs.

Stone sinks Old sinks, usually shallow and frequently used

to create miniature gardens for alpine plants, small bulbs and miniature conifers.

Strawberry barrels A novel way to grow strawberries in large barrels.

Summer-flowering bedding plants Plants raised from seeds sown in gentle warmth in early spring, slowly acclimatized to outdoor conditions and planted into containers when the risk of frost has passed. In autumn, they are discarded.

Tender perennials Perennial plants such as pelargoniums and most fuchsias that are not sufficiently hardy in temperate climates to be left outside throughout winter.

Terraces Open, paved areas immediately outside a house. Sometimes, they are on several levels and united by flights of steps.

Terracotta (also terra-cotta): A hardy, brownish-red material formed of clay, fine sand and, occasionally, pulverized pottery waste. This is made into containers - usually unglazed - for plants.

Top-dressing When shrubs and small trees and in containers cannot be repotted, to provide them with fresh nutrients the

surface soil in the container is removed in spring and replaced with fresh. Ensure that the roots of plants are not damaged.

Tree A woody plant with a single, clear stem between the roots and lowest branches.

Urn A vase of varying shape and ornamentation made of glassfibre, metal, plastic or reconstituted stone. Because of the limited amount of compost they can hold, they are mainly used for summer-flowering plants.

Verandah (also Veranda): A term derived from India, describing a gallery at ground-level and on one side of a house (sometimes surrounding it). The roof slopes to shed water and the sides are partly or wholly open on the garden side.

Versailles planter A large, square-sided container originated at Versailles, France. Early ones were made of lead or slate, while modern types are glassfibre or wood.

Vermiculite A moisture-retentive material added to compost.

INDEX